★ ★ ★ ★ ★

UNDERWAY

ONE FAMILY'S GUIDE TO SURVIVING BOOT CAMP

★ ★ ★ ★ ★

By Ruel Knudson

First Edition: July 2024

This book is not endorsed by or affiliated with the United States Navy.

ISBN: 979-8-9902507-0-3 (paperback)
ISBN: 979-8-9902507-1-0 (hardcover)
ISBN: 979-8-9902507-2-7 (ebook)

Printed in the United States of America

Dedicated to the ones who love the ones who serve.

Contents

Preface

Our family does not have a military tradition. While there are members of our extended family who have served, military service was completely new territory for us.

So how did two of my children decide to enlist in the armed services? Quite simply, economics. Like many people, we struggled. For a long time, I was the sole provider for my family, and every cent was accounted for. At times, we barely kept a roof over our heads and food on the table. There was nothing left to save. My wife and I could provide for our family's well-being, but I could not secure a future for our children.

My kids knew that the best chance for a life determined by their dreams and ambitions lay in education. But to afford that, they would need to get scholarships or join the military. I urged them away from financing, student loans, and starting out their adult lives burdened by debt. The military was an option that we always kept on the table. They joined ROTC and Sea Cadets programs, preparing themselves in case they chose to join the military to pay for school.

They chose to serve. Not to pay for school. Not for the leg up. It turned out the military wasn't something they had to do; it was something they wanted to do. The college benefits were a big plus, but that wasn't what drove them.

What surprises me most is how much they love it. I wouldn't be surprised to find either of them serving a full 20-year career in the military. After all, why not retire with a pension at 38? I can only imagine the opportunities and freedom they could have at an age when I inspected every bill like it was a loaded gun. It's enough to make you reexamine your own life choices.

I don't know if coming from a military family, or if I had served, would have helped navigate boot camp or the graduation ceremony at Great Lakes. What I did know is that this new world wasn't just foreign, it was intimidating. We constantly felt unprepared. Information was everywhere, but questions weren't always easy to answer. The paradoxical resource of the internet had so much information to offer that it renders itself nearly useless.

I thought I might just be bad at this whole military family thing, but I wasn't alone. I met other families at Great Lakes who felt the same way. All we had were social media groups and websites. Many of these were helpful, but they could only answer a question that was asked. What about the questions we didn't think to ask? There was an enormous vacancy of information. We did not know what we did not know. There was no guidebook. No one was telling their story.

It's not surprising for an author to want to solve this problem by writing about it. Before I left Great Lakes, the seeds for this book had already been planted. This happens to me a lot, but I usually resist the initial urge to act on these ideas. Most of my "great ideas" evaporate. Waiting is my filter. It's the meter by which I measure if something needs to be written. No good idea withers in my mind.

Then there are the stories that nag at me. They dig in and don't let go. I wake up thinking about them, and I go to bed wishing paragraphs of text would stop invading my attempts at sleep. They bite, claw, and needle in and out of my thoughts, begging to be let in. Those stories refuse to evaporate. They grow until the shadow of them can't be ignored. Those are the stories I write.

This is one of those stories.

Part 1 – Our Story

"The Navy has both a tradition and a future — and we look with pride and confidence in both directions."

- Admiral George Anderson

01. Goodbye

I remember feeling a sinking sensation in my stomach—a sense of impending emptiness, as if any step forward would lead to failure. But with this feeling, there was also a glimmer of opportunity, an electric excitement, and a growing anticipation. Embracing this meant I could smile, and bask in the warm glow of a promising new future for my daughter. Yet even within this hopefulness, fear and uncertainty remained.

We found ourselves standing in a strip mall parking lot, the type of place where the government pays cheap rent for storefronts that no one else really wants. On the southern end, there was a gas station where a panhandler was looking to scrape together enough change for a pack of cigarettes. To the north, a collection of rusting shopping carts with blue plastic handles stood lonely and forgotten among a few cars, all surrounded by litter.

This was the "other side" of the strip mall, hidden away from the main stores. The storefront spaces were affordable because they existed out of sight from Walmart, Lowe's, and other major retailers. Tucked between a few family-owned specialty shops is where our children go to sign up with good ol' Uncle Sam. We said our goodbyes in an ugly place where the occasional weeds desperately tried to grow through cracks in the blacktop.

I looked at this young woman, wishing I could see the simple child she once was. Adulthood had arrived too soon. What happened to the innocent little girl whose boundless optimism was so comforting? I wanted to rewind time to those years of blissful innocence, where clumsy awkwardness was blindly accepted and humor was found in things that mature adults found horribly embarrassing. Why couldn't the molded sculpture of adulthood be returned to a pliable mound of unformed adolescent clay?

I wished to go back to those years not to correct mistakes or to make different choices, but to relive them, slowing down time like a replay. Perhaps I would pause it, delaying the future a bit longer. I wanted to hold onto a time before she transformed into a confident young adult, saying goodbye to her family as she embarked on a great adventure.

I am so proud of her.

However, my pride is tempered by skepticism. No matter how intelligent, kind, and strong she may be, I know she is human and flawed. And her accomplishments were achieved under the safe umbrella of loving and careful parents.

Our children were supported by us. We held them up and helped them reach as high as they were willing to go. We allowed for failure and consequences, even as we ensured these outcomes wouldn't be too devastating or would prevent our children from picking themselves up and trying again. Our family acted as a safety net: when our children fell, they never hit the ground too hard.

Despite this, all I see is the strength and wisdom of a person far beyond her years, and I am in awe. She is unequalled in her goodness and potential. My kid, the person who said her goodbyes to her family on a cracked blacktop parking lot, is special—but then all three of my children are special. Her older brother serves in the United States Air Force, and her little sister, born with spina bifida and literally looking up to her sister from a wheelchair, is still in high school, with her own aspirations to take her beyond our home and into an exciting career in psychology. All three are strong, amazing, and unique. No one compares to my kids.

It occurred to me then that I am not the first parent to feel this way, and I certainly won't be the last. I am just another father in a long line of parents who have stood in front of that office, beaming with pride while secretly wishing this day had not come. I am the latest who looked at their child and saw someone about to become a sailor while thinking two conflicting thoughts:

I am so proud to be her dad.

Not my kid. Not today. Not tomorrow. Maybe never. It is too soon.

I understand these feelings may seem contradictory. How can I be so excited for her future, ready for her to make her place in the world, and yet also want her to never grow up? I accept these feelings as true, honest, and real. I know they seem to be incompatible emotional states, and yet I allow them to coexist. This is who I am: a proud father who can't wait to see the future, while yearning for my children to remain forever young. I was saying goodbye to my daughter, soon to become a sailor in the greatest navy in history, and I secretly hoped she would change her mind and ask to come back home with us.

The truth is that I am not bound by any specific set of emotions. There are no requirements dictating what I should feel. Some parents may regret their children's decision to serve, while others may come from military families with hopes that their kid will have a long and illustrious career. Some, like us, view the armed forces as presenting an opportunity we cannot provide.

Whatever our feelings about this new path, we can accept them as genuine and valid emotions. We need to own them. No other person gets to define what is right or wrong about how we feel. And for those of us who may not be thrilled about our loved one's choice, we should strive to be proud of them—proud of who they are, and proud of where they are headed.

Being the parent, family, friend, spouse, or loved one of a person who chooses to serve in the armed forces brings a range of complex and diverse emotions that defy classification. No one else can tell me these feelings are wrong. But for me, someone who loved these little creatures and continued to love them as they grow into adults who answer this call, I never had a choice: I just love them.

This was the second time I found myself in the parking lot of a recruiting office, saying goodbye to one of my children. Years ago, my oldest had left this same lot for Air Force Basic Training. Now we were here for my daughter, who was leaving to join the Navy. It was the same poorly maintained slab of concrete from years before; the vehicles scattered across the lot might have been different, but the scene was identical.

As we took pictures, smiled our best smiles, hugged, and said our goodbyes, a curious thought nagged at me. It was the same persistent thought I had been suppressing for days, demanding to be acknowledged, refusing to be ignored:

This shouldn't be as difficult as last time.

But it was even harder now, because I understood what this truly involved. Everything was changing. Even if she changed her mind, stayed home, and gave up on this path, there was no going back to the way things were. She had grown up. Moving on was the only thing that would ever happen. Tomorrow had arrived. The choices we made had determined the outcome, one way or another.

I was surprised by our near absence of tears. Our daughter stood straight and proud, ready to move forward, although still slightly hesitant about the next step. Mom's eyes were wet, but her cheeks were dry. Only Little Sister was crying; she was clearly trying to fight off the tears, but they overwhelmed her. She didn't say anything. I wondered what she would tell me if I asked. Was she seeing a tomorrow where her sister, her best friend, was no longer home? There would be no more daily breakfast conversations with her. Weekly movie nights with the four of us would now only be the three of us. Our nightly dinner conversations would no longer include her voice, or her laughter at bad jokes and puns. The secret conversations meant only for sisters, when mom and dad were out of earshot, must have seemed to be ending forever. How cavernous must the emptiness feel for a young girl, the remaining child who would be the last to leave?

I could have asked her, but it wouldn't have been fair. These emotions were so complex. How could anyone articulate them while in the middle of experiencing them? Only after looking back and confronting my own thoughts on that day—reflecting on them, dissecting them, and piecing them back together into some coherent form—was I able to reflect on the feelings I wrestled with. So that day, instead of words, we silently acknowledged each other's acceptance of what was happening. And while we all shared a sense of loss, each in our own way, I could also see how proud we all were; I could feel the pride within me, and it was overflowing.

Then our to-be sailor got into a car with a group of strangers, and they drove off to places I had never been, to do things I had never done, and to be a part of a world I would never know.

We watched them leave, driving off and merging into the morning traffic. It didn't take long before they were swallowed by the river of vehicles. I hated those cars, their drivers, the routine lives they were carrying on, their ability to just go through the motions and get through another day. I resented their normalcy—their trips to work, the gas station, or a fast-food place to buy some overpriced processed garbage.

I envied them for not having to say goodbye to the

people they loved, for knowing what would happen next. They lived in the comfort of day-to-day monotony, not aware that the car joining the line of traffic was taking away a child, leaving a father, a mother, and a sister standing on a cracked blacktop; they simply absorbed them into the flow, carrying her away toward a future without us.

It was the same when my son left for basic training. I didn't think it could feel any different for me. Normally, I was excited about the adventures my children had; I shared in their enthusiastic embrace of the new courses they embarked on. But a part of me felt left out, unable to experience it with them.

My wife and I encouraged our kids to try new things, seek out new experiences, explore possibilities, and take ownership and responsibility for their lives. Until now, they had been children, and our guidance and encouragement were accompanied by the comfort of knowing that if something went wrong, we were there. Not being in a place to offer security left a hole in me, filling me with anxiety over the uncertainty.

This wasn't a rational fear, but I couldn't dismiss it: it incessantly gnawed at the back of my mind. It contradicted everything I expected of myself as a parent. It implied a lack of trust in my children and their abilities, as if I hadn't prepared them to be adults. I questioned my own motivations as a parent. I second-guessed their decisions.

Once again, I found myself accepting these unfair feelings as real and honest. If I refused to fight them, they wouldn't interfere with the choices my children were making. Accepting them didn't mean I had to embrace them; accepting them just silenced them, pushing them back into the recesses of my mind where they could only whisper.

These concerns may seem irrational when they first arise, but they are a natural reaction to accepting an unknown future. I felt as if I was relinquishing any further control or influence over my children as they became adults. This is something all parents must do as their kids move on to their own independent lives. Sometimes this transition is gradual, and for others, it is the span of time between arriving at a recruiter's office and watching the car carry your child off to training. It hits you in places you weren't expecting, and it hits hard. However, it is a fallacy.

Sure, I won't have the daily and direct impact on my children I was used to—but as they grow up, we are not cast aside, dismissed, or forgotten. We aren't made irrelevant. The nature of our influence has changed, but it has not been removed. *That* is the struggle. This is why I refuse to embrace the fears and give them strength: the feelings might be real, but where they come from—the place where the maturing of our relationships changes how our connection looks—is trying to convince me something horrible is happening. This is the lie in the fear. Nothing horrible is happening. Change is constant, and for my children, this change is good.

Acceptance does not bring peace, and it does not bring happiness. Saying goodbye didn't cause a chapter to close, and we didn't get back into our car ready to turn any pages. We just left, three of us instead of four, heading off to face the first day of our new normal.

For the life of me, I can't remember the drive home. I don't remember the rest of my day with any more clarity than a list of bullet points. I went home, and then I went to work. I came home after work. We had dinner. We missed her. The only remarkable thing about the day was her leaving, her absence. Whatever remained, she took it with her when that car drove away.

In the grand scope of this journey my child is taking, the day she left was the worst. It was the day I volunteered to be the parent of an adult. We relinquished control, and she took it for herself. And while she may be joining the

Navy, thus signing away some of her independence, it was still her choice to do it—and it will be her own strength, intelligence, perseverance, and character that determine her success. All we had to do was refuse to interfere, to support her and the choice she made.

I'm glad we did. At times, I didn't think we would be able to do this. Sometimes, I wanted to pull back, slow down, or take a different path. On the day she left, I came the closest to stopping all of this from happening. But I didn't. Truth be told, I don't think I could have stopped it. I take a small amount of pride in myself, and in all of us, for letting it happen—for standing by her and saying our good-byes with love, hope, and the promise of our support.

02. Letters and Calls

There was a lot we needed to consider in the lead-up to our daughter's departure for boot camp. We spoke with recruiters, checked social media groups, read articles, and watched videos. At first, we felt prepared. However, we soon realized there were things we had forgotten to finalize before our daughter left.

We wondered what we should do if someone in the family got sick, injured, or even died. How would we let her know, and when? Are the rules different for close friends or extended family? Would this make it harder for her to finish training, knowing but not able to do anything about it? Leaving her out of any news felt wrong, but at this point, asking her how we would handle this would make her instantly assume something had happened. This was an important detail to overlook, and the threat of having to deal with this loomed over her entire time at boot camp.

We also assumed Mom would be the primary point of contact, but we didn't formally establish this. As a result, we all watched our phones like hawks, never knowing if a strange area code, private number, or pay phone would be her. Normally, our phones had the "Do Not Disturb" mode turned on at night for everyone except close family or friends, in case of emergencies. Now, we turned that feature off. Fortunately, we only received a few spam calls during boot camp. The uncertainty around regular calls and when we might receive them added to our fear. Every time our phones rang, the world stopped and we held our breaths, waiting for the person on the phone to let us know if she had called.

We also continued to receive mail for her marked

"Navy Federal" and regarding college opportunities. We should have set up a protocol for holding or forwarding these letters. Instead, we just bundled them together with the expectation that we would deal with them later. I don't think we ever dealt with them at all.

Despite these oversights, we were ahead on other issues. I made sure her civilian bank account and credit card accounts were taken care of. Before she left, she changed the passwords to something I could use. She had already canceled her recurring bills, so the accounts were easy to maintain; still, twice a month I logged in and checked each account, looking for anything she might have missed, or anything suspicious.

Any important documentation she didn't need for the Navy or boot camp was packed into a binder and kept in our fireproof box. It was secure and safe while also accessible to both parents. Once she was settled at Accession Training (also known as "A" School) following boot camp graduation, or even later, we could hand everything back over to her.

More importantly, we set an expectation for communication. We had already asked her how often she would like to receive letters. It didn't really matter: Mom had already decided she would write daily. She might not send a letter every day, but if she were to mail something once a week, it would contain a week's worth of correspondence, and there was nothing she could say about that.

For my part, I told our daughter that I held no expectations about the quality or frequency of letters and calls from her. She had a job to do, and the job would be difficult; she might not have the time or energy to write letters. The most important thing was for her to focus on her training and get it done. After all, I knew she loved me, and I knew she wanted to communicate with me. While I wanted letters, it was more important for her to succeed at training. So I absolved her of feeling obligated to write to me. If it came down to choosing between sleep or writing a letter, she should choose sleep.

Mom's response to this was that I needed to shut my face. She expected and wanted letters, even if they were few and far between. There was also the matter of other people writing to her. She might have teachers, friends, grandparents, or siblings sending her well-wishes and support, and these people should receive a response. These letters wouldn't be as frequent as our correspondence, so a simple "thanks for writing" wouldn't be too difficult. Our recruit should appreciate the love sent her way and be grateful enough to send a reply.

Even with these expectations set, we still had to come to terms with the one-directional nature of communication with a recruit during boot camp. There were a few phone calls after she left the recruiting office. She let us know when she had returned to Military Entrance Processing Station (MEPS). From there, a group of them boarded a bus that took them to the airport; we received a phone call from there, and then she was on a plane. Upon our daughter's arrival at O'Hare International Airport in Chicago, Mom received a brief phone call.

Then silence. Hours of nothing as my mind filled with unanswerable questions. Where were they? What were they doing? What was happening?

What went wrong?

We were told to expect a final "I arrived" call when she made it to Recruit Training Command (RTC), the official name for boot camp. We thought this would be a quick trip from the airport to the base. Of course, we had no real idea of what we should expect, and the long silence was horrible. When the call came, it was very late. Hours had gone by. Little Sister and I were asleep. Mom received the call, and it was even more brief and terse than we thought it would be.

It was as advertised, and yet we were shockingly unprepared for it.

"I've arrived. I'm safe. I love you. Goodbye."

There was no time to wake us—it was over so fast. This was all we would get for a long time. We wouldn't hear her voice or receive a letter for what felt like an eternity.

The next morning, I received an update from my wife. She had had only about fifteen seconds on the phone with our daughter. Our daughter told us much later that there had been trouble with her phone, but at the time, we had no way of knowing what was happening.

With so few words from her, I wondered what she wanted to convey. I could hear her voice in my head, telling me she was terrified. She had made a terrible mistake. She wanted to come home. I imagined grabbing the keys and rushing to Naval Station Great Lakes in the family rescue mobile, driving a hundred miles an hour to save my child from Sergeant Shouty-Pants and the Navy.

Instead, I looked at my wife and hoped she couldn't read my thoughts or see my concern written on my face. I didn't want anyone to know that I felt like I had made a huge mistake by allowing this to happen.

Days and weeks passed, Mom and me starting each conversation at the end of our day with "Have you heard from her?" as if we wouldn't have immediately informed each other if one of us had received a call. With no news, I painfully imagined all the terrible things that could go wrong at boot camp. It was an utterly frustrating silence.

We had anticipated this, but it didn't make it any easier. For at least ten weeks, she would be training, studying, and developing herself into a sailor. She was preparing to join the men and women who make up the most essential elements of the world's largest, most powerful, and most technologically advanced Navy; this would not be a walk in the park. She would face trials and tests; she would fail and rise again, and eventually become the type of sailor our country could be proud of.

As she met these challenges, we would be an essential part of her success, keeping her motivated and connected to the love and security that must have seemed so far away. There would be moments of fear and uncertainty. She would have doubts, and the desire to give up, come home, and abandon this effort would be incredibly strong. She might even seriously consider sacrificing her future goals and walk away from this forever. Many had arrived at RTC with grand ambitions, only to discover that it was a trial they were not capable of overcoming. She could be one of those people.

She wouldn't be alone during her training. She would find support and assistance from the other recruits. There would be allies and friends to lift her up when she felt over-whelmed. But those people wouldn't be us. They wouldn't know her the way we do. It wouldn't be our voices. We would need to send our voices to her, shouting encourage-ment through ink and paper from a thousand miles away.

So we wrote letters. If she had been interested in sports, I would have sent her sports scores; if she had been into video games, I would have tried them and shared my im-pressions with her. Instead, I focused on our shared inter-ests: books, movies, and superheroes. I wrote her updates and anecdotes, sharing some of the mundane aspects of our lives while also sprinkling in funnier and more remarkable moments.

I shared my thoughts on shows that I thought she might want to watch after completing her training. Sometimes it was news I hoped she would find interesting. Most of the time, I sent rambling snapshots of life at home, along with bad jokes and utter nonsense. After all, the world was still turning, and these little bits of life at home were the things we might have discussed over coffee or dinner if she had been home with us.

Above all, I let her know I was there for her. I was proud of her. I knew she could finish this.

Mom sent her memes and jokes she found on the internet, the kinds of things she would have texted her on any normal day. Sometimes it was just a printed-out picture. All of this was in addition to the love and support only a mother could provide.

While Little Sister wasn't as prolific, she did write a letter once or twice a week. Sometimes it was at Mom's urging. I don't know what was written in those pages, but I can imagine our recruit reading them, hearing Little Sister's voice as she scanned the words across the page, a broad smile spreading on her face.

I believe the letters helped. We never discussed them after she graduated. I don't know if there were days when she felt alone, hopeless, or dejected. I was afraid there would be a time when things were terrible, and she returned to her bunk regretting everything. If such a time were to come, our words of love and encouragement would be there when she needed us the most.

When it all comes down to it, we may have sent too few letters. I knew we could never send too many. She might have been too busy to read everything we sent. She could have stored them away, unread and forgotten. She could have simply thrown them in the trash. What happened to the letters she received was up to her. But if no letters had come, she couldn't wish them into existence. She couldn't choose for a letter to arrive that was never written or sent to her. Not having the letters she needed would have been our failure.

In return, the letters from our recruit were short and infrequent. I didn't have any expectations, but Mom often expressed her wish to hear more from her. Truthfully, I felt the same way. We had also anticipated this, and once again our mental preparation hadn't been enough—it would never have been enough. There was little news or information about what was happening, and we were craving more. The longer it took, the more anxious we became for any updates.

Days turned into weeks, and still silence. This became the true test of our confidence in her. As a parent, I found myself imagining the worst possible scenarios. She was a thousand miles away, and she could be struggling through her training and miserable in every aspect of it. She could be injured or sick. She might be alone, disliked, and struggling without anyone's help.

She might be afraid.

We had no choice but to wait. Every letter involved a battle with the urge to pressure her to write back. Any communication we received was both a blessing and a curse: it was nice to hear something, but there was so little said. So many questions remained unanswered, and new questions arose with each brief exchange.

I wanted so much and received so little in return. I tried finding solace in the shared silence; since no one else heard from her more often than the others, it meant she was likely too busy to reach out. I tried keeping the faith that nothing else had gone wrong.

One thing I refused to do was let her know how the silence affected us. I didn't want to add to the stress, pressure, and challenges she was already facing. I wanted her to stay focused, feel supported, and know she was loved. This burden would be mine, and I would happily carry it for her.

In truth, there were many reasons for the limited correspondence, and none of those reasons was a lack of desire to write back or call us. I could only imagine, but I think home was something recruits thought about a lot. But finding enough time and energy to write was a different matter altogether.

There is also the lost art of letter-writing itself. Some people simply don't have the focus or skill to write a letter. It's strange to realize how most communication nowadays is either verbal or in short text messages. Expressing our thoughts in a letter is something people don't do anymore, and some people may not feel comfortable in trying.

In the end, we received three batches of letters, and each batch had a letter for each of us, including for me. They were little things, hastily scrawled on small slips of paper. Three more letters than I expected. A thousand less than I wanted. I considered myself lucky to have received any.

Each letter was specifically written for the individual it was sent to and covered a different topic. Mom, Little Sister, and I shared the letters with each other, filling in gaps and expanding our shared understanding of her life at RTC. It wasn't much, but we cherished every word. These glimpses into her world told us that things were hard, but she was doing well. She was healthy and she was strong.

Recruits were also given opportunities to make phone calls in a large room filled with small sit-down phone booths. I expected her to be careful with her words; she was within earshot of other recruits and the leadership, so if there were specific problems with individuals or concerns about training beyond her own shortcomings, she had to express them cautiously.

We learned she had been tapped for leadership. She was the Starboard Watch Section Leader, which gave her the thankless task of organizing the various watch schedules. Of course, this was bound to attract criticism and accusations of favoritism from other recruits. A perfectly balanced watch schedule would still appear unfair to someone who found themselves on an unfavorable watch time. Watch duty essentially translated into busy work, which meant less free time and rest.

There would be no winning at this task, and yet it was hers. While it didn't help her popularity, it gave her two things she needed: confidence in her skills to organize and maintain a task, and the knowledge that the Navy, her direct leadership, and her fellow watch leaders supported her. The leaders valued her, and when conflicts escalated, the Navy shut it down and expressed their confidence in their choice of Watch Leader.

This drama unfolded over a few calls, spaced weeks apart. When it was at its lowest point, we could only listen and try to express our love and support without it sounding like a series of empty platitudes. But how could we express more than that? We had no real understanding of what she was going through.

I had nothing relevant to offer her: I was never in the military, and even if I had been, the Navy had changed a lot from any period when I might have been at boot camp. What little I could say was the one truth I thought mattered: she was strong, intelligent, and capable. The Navy decided she could do the job. She didn't ask for it. She didn't want it. Someone looked at the recruits and decided that she had the skills required for the task. Someone believed in her.

We later found out that two other recruits had volunteered for the job, but they were unsuccessful despite their best efforts. At that point, the leadership decided to take charge of the decision, instead of leaving it to the recruits to volunteer. The job required skill, organization, and attention to detail; they couldn't rely on assumptions of capability. She was their first choice for the job.

She accepted the responsibility and, along with the Port Watch Section Leader, transformed an empty office into a staging area for organizing and planning the watches. Others noticed and adopted their operational methods. When problems increased with the recruits she had assigned watches to, the leadership intervened and made it clear who they supported and why: she was the Starboard Section Watch Leader, and that wouldn't change. Her decisions were final, and dissent wouldn't be tolerated.

While this sounded promising, it was evident her anxiety around the situation persisted. However, I felt more at ease knowing that the Navy saw her as having value. Meanwhile, the slow progress and limited communication caused my anxiety to build over weeks of sparse calls. It was difficult to remain optimistic; my confidence in her never wavered, but it also required trust in people I hadn't met and an institution with which I had no real experience. These unknown factors were significant and ambiguous enough to keep me awake at night, imagining all the ways things could go wrong.

As we approached the end, we began to notice changes in her mood and expectations. Battle Stations was the next and final challenge, a sort of final exam for the sailors. It was the culmination of everything they had learned. Their skills and knowledge should now be strong enough to pass this test, yet the uncertainty regarding unit cohesion added an extra layer of stress.

In the lead-up to Battle Stations, the phone conversations had become more frequent but were dominated by the exam. Then came the final call before the test. She sounded nervous, but excited. At that point, we could only wait for the all-important "I'm a Sailor" call.

It was like waiting for Christmas—we knew it was approaching, we knew it would be amazing, we knew there was no way this could possibly go wrong. We had come to the end. But there was no guarantee Battle Stations would go well: it depended on all of the sailors working together, doing their best. Success was not entirely up to an individual recruit. But if things did go wrong, it would only result in a delay until graduation. The recruits who didn't pass would be ASMO'd, or given an Assignment Memorandum Order that would reassign them to another division, where they could attempt to qualify again. So, failure was essentially just a setback, which could be frustrating but didn't mean they couldn't become sailors.

While this may not seem high-stakes, the significance of passing was immense. I could hear the conflict between our daughter's confidence and her more cautious uncertainty. It was contagious: intellectually, I knew she would do well, but her nervousness seeped in. As we waited for the next call, the anticipation continued to build.

And then it came. The pride and overwhelming sense of accomplishment in her voice was unforgettable. They had done it.

Not only had they succeeded, but the experience itself would forever be a part of her adventure. The brief descriptions she was allowed to share, together with the few videos we found online, revealed a grueling and exhilarating series of tests involving basic sailor skills, firefighting, stopping leaks, life-saving challenges, rescue simulations, and more. There was even a re-creation of the attack on the USS *Cole* included in the test. The fact that my child not only faced these challenges but triumphed over them, enduring hardships I could only imagine, was humbling for me.

Of course, this doesn't mean everything was smooth sailing. Yes, graduation was just around the corner, and they had overcome the biggest challenge of their training. But there were still a few tests remaining. I got the sense that passing Battle Stations wasn't just a major exam: it gave our sailor a newfound appreciation for her own abilities, as well as confidence in the skill and talent of her fellow sailors. Any remaining tasks were mere formalities to them; they had already endured the worst and emerged smiling, proud, and assured. They now knew who they were: they were no longer recruits—they were officially sailors in the U.S. Navy.

03. Logistics

Planning for Pass in Review (PIR), the RTC graduation ceremony, began before our sailor left for boot camp. Her recruiter was very clear that it would be impossible to guarantee a definitive date for graduation, although he didn't provide much information on why.

In hindsight, it is clear why recruiters might not be transparent about the graduation date. It's not that they are hiding anything, but rather that the factors contributing to the graduation date are sometimes out of the control of the Navy or the recruit. This can add stress and insecurity around an already daunting life change. Given the number of unforeseeable factors that can affect graduation, it is best to address them if or when they become an issue.

For instance, PIR may be delayed if the recruit is assigned to a performance division, which is usually reserved for recruits with a musical background and experience. These recruits are provided with an instrument or given a role in this division, which performs at graduation ceremonies for training groups—including their own. Some people recommend avoiding being assigned to a performance division because it can add extra responsibilities and delay the PIR date; the graduation may be pushed back by a few weeks, depending on how long it takes to gather enough musical recruits to fill the division. Despite the delays, both my son and daughter were part of performance divisions, and they loved the experience.

Another factor that is likely to affect the graduation date is the recruit's performance and ability to reach milestones. Delays may occur due to illness, injury, or other incidents, although even these are rarely problematic enough to cause a delay in graduation. In severe cases, the recruit may be ASMO'd to another division, requiring them to repeat previous stages of training.

Illness can be a difficult obstacle for sailors, as large groups of people are living and working in close quarters. Common issues include colds, the flu, and viral infections such as pink eye. Unless the illness is severe, missing a day or two of training is not enough to cause a delay; however, if the illness persists, the recruit may be moved to another division once they recover.

Despite these challenges, it is rare for sailors to not finish training. The Navy does not want recruits to fail: the time spent by instructors, fellow recruits, and the individual is extensive, and no one wants to see that effort wasted. There is also a financial cost to the Navy, recruits, and their families. People often only see the incentives and the sometimes aggressive recruiting methods employed by the military to get people to join. They may forget about the academic, health, and mental requirements that must be met and evaluated before a recruit even makes it to RTC. The Navy wants to ensure that the effort and money put into a recruit will pay off. The recruiting process, ASVAB testing, and MEPS are all there to determine if the individual meets a minimum set of standards. This helps ensure that the recruit can be expected to succeed at boot camp and that they have a solid foundation to build on, and they are used to weed out anyone that may not make it through RTC. Because the recruit has already demonstrated their ability to become a sailor before arriving at RTC, the Navy is incentivized to preserve their viability. If a recruit fails to meet the requirements to proceed through training, they will be moved to another training set or even a different division, which will delay graduation.

While being ASMO'd may cause difficulties in scheduling and planning a trip to attend the graduation, it is not necessarily a bad thing. Some may see it as a failure, but I choose to see it as similar to getting held back in grade school: it gives a struggling sailor an opportunity to try again, using their accumulated knowledge and skills and reinforced by their previous experience, to push through and meet the requirements. In the end, this will make them better sailors.

What was more important for us was how we would have communicated with our sailor if she were to inform us of being held back. We would have kept our disappointment with the delays to ourselves and let our sailor explain what happened, providing her an opportunity to express her disappointment or frustration. Then, we would have pointed out the benefits and opportunities of being AS-MO'd and made sure to give her our support and confidence in her ultimate success.

The watchwords are patience and understanding: any shared thoughts or feelings must reinforce our confidence in her, the hard work she has done, and the accomplishments she has already achieved, while also promoting a sense of purpose and potential. We must remind her, and ourselves, that the Navy knows she can do this. Over two hundred years of training sailors instills in us a faith in her ability to continue, finish RTC, and serve among the best and brightest in our nation's impressive roster of men and women who have answered this call.

While we were not excited about delays complicating our travel arrangements, we still had to prepare for the possibility. Any postponement can impose a significant hardship on families who want to attend the graduation ceremony. It was important that we planned carefully to ensure that none of us would miss the event, but there were other factors that had to be considered beyond the financial costs.

Shortly before my daughter left for boot camp, I started a new job. There I was, trying to convince my employer that

I am a dependable member of the team and dedicated to my new position in their company, while also informing them that at some point in about two months, I would need some time off for a long weekend. I provided the expected date and explained that this date may be moved. I was asking for time off work within my first ninety days of employment. That is never a good way to start a job.

I felt like an idiot, shooting myself in the foot, or at the very least putting myself in a position where I already owed my employers a favor. Despite their assurances, I already had the deck stacked against me. I was asking a lot while also trying to make sure nothing else would go wrong— hoping that Mom, Little Sister, and I would not get sick, suffer an injury, or face some other hardships that would require further time off. Any appointments I had with doctors needed to be rescheduled; any non-essential events I would have to miss. Work came first. I couldn't let anything else go wrong, or I'd risk my employer having doubts about me.

To complicate things further, the amorphous mark on the calendar seemed to remain perpetually vague and wavering, refusing to define itself until just a few weeks before it was announced as a likely certainty. A constant stream of "should be" and "probably" always accompanied the date. Even when it was announced, it always threatened to change, creating a constant cloud of uncertainty and stress that loomed over us.

I kept wondering: If the date moved too far in one direction or another, would my time off at work be available to me? Would I have to stay home and miss the graduation, just to keep the job? Would it be worth risking this job to see her standing proud among her fellow sailors, to be there for her at such an important milestone in her adventure into her own future?

The conversation about what we would do if the trip

conflicted with our jobs was something we avoided, as if discussing it might invite it to happen. Personally, I felt that if it came down to it, I would have to choose my job over the trip. There were no guarantees that I would find work elsewhere, or that we could survive without my income. It was an unspoken expectation that we had to prioritize the family, even if it meant sacrificing the participation of one or both parents. Our goal was to do everything we could to avoid having to make that choice.

Even before my first day at work, I made sure to keep my managers informed about the situation. Once I started working, I took every occasion to remind them that I still didn't have a specific graduation date: every timesheet I turned in, every meeting with supervisors and coworkers, and every conversation concerning my upcoming goals or training were all used as opportunities to remind everyone of my situation.

When it became clear that the graduation date would fall on Veterans Day weekend, I formally requested time off, knowing that I still might have to change it later. I continued to provide updates, and I reassured my employer that I would inform them as soon as I had any new information. By doing this, I lessened the impact of any changes; my team could plan around a certain level of uncertainty as long as I kept them informed.

Slowly, my confidence grew, and the looming shadow dimmed; the stress from the uncertainty ebbed, and I felt sure that any sudden shifts in the date would be manageable. I wouldn't have to choose between my daughter's RTC graduation and employment. With my job secure, all we really needed to do was start scheduling the necessities of the trip.

We live in Florida, so if we had to drive to Chicago, the trip wouldn't be too terrible. But the limited time off from work meant this wouldn't be a practical option. Sure, the drive was something we could make in a day or so, even including stops to rest and eat, but we would be exhausted when we arrived. Also, there would be very little time for additional preparation for the visit. So, we looked for flights.

Air travel isn't cheap. Furthermore, adding on the ability to cancel or change our flights if needed incurred additional fees. However, rolling the dice on losing the entire ticket price wasn't an option: we paid the upcharges, knowing that if things went sideways, we would have some kind of insurance that would help soften the financial blow. Furthermore, we booked our flights within weeks of our planned trip, which means the ticket prices were further inflated. Normally, our trips are better planned, and we can usually pay better prices. Unfortunately, the fluidity of the graduation date made it difficult to book earlier. If the prices ballooned any higher, we were prepared to rent a car and make the drive, even if that meant we would arrive exhausted and unrested.

We reserved a rental car for getting around in Illinois. Predicting that one of America's largest cities would also be fed by numerous toll roads, I ordered a toll transponder that was compatible with both Florida and Illinois tolls. The transponder only cost $25; even adding in the cost of tolls, the total would still be cheaper than paying the fees rental car providers charge.

Our lodging needs were easier to fulfill than expected. Our initial thought was to use Airbnb or a similar service, as we had done when my son graduated from Air Force training in Texas. These spaces are typically more spacious and come with full kitchens and other amenities to make accommodations more comfortable. They are great if you want a more homelike experience, especially if you plan on doing any cooking. However, the Navy has restrictions on the number of people allowed to attend the graduation ceremony. Since there would only be three of us, plus the sailor, we didn't feel the need to rent a large space, especially considering how little we expected to use it. Hotels are expensive, but often very comfortable; however, there was a risk of not being able to change the reservation dates. In addition, hotels often adjust rates based on occupancy, so a great rate one day may not be so great if we needed to make a last-minute change.

Fortunately, we found a solution available through the Navy. The Navy Exchange Service Command (NEXCOM) owns and operates various Navy Exchange (NEX) retail stores and other services exclusively for military members, their families, retired military personnel, and authorized civilians who work or operate on military bases. While most people expect NEXCOM to operate stores, uniform, and barber services exclusively on or near bases, they also operate Navy Lodge Hotels, and one of these is conveniently located near the base where our sailor was.

My initial concern was that the place might be more of a motel than a hotel. After all, there are certain expectations in the civilian world of the standards of military "benefits": sure, they are available and reliable, but a Navy barber is not the first place that comes to mind when my wife wants to get her hair done. However, in our case, price was more important than convenience.

Everything looked great on the website. The images showed nice rooms with enough space and amenities to meet our needs. Additionally, they had the necessary accommodations for Little Sister's accessibility needs, including plenty of room for her wheelchair. As any family with a wheelchair user knows, the quality of "accessibility" can vary greatly, from acceptable to barely usable or even dangerous.

Furthermore, they have a generous cancellation policy. We had the option to cancel or change our stay up to twenty-four hours before our scheduled arrival. To be fair, many hotels offer similar policies, but they can be unpredictable, with extensive fine print and additional fees for cancellations. The location, price, and policies of the Navy Lodge seemed to be more accommodating to military families, which makes sense since it is administered by the Navy (via NEXCOM).

With our lodging, vehicle, and travel plans in place, we still had to consider what to bring on the trip. Due to our sailor's rate—i.e., her job and rank in the Navy—we had some understanding of how much free time she would have. While nothing was guaranteed, the holiday weekend and her Accession Training being in another state made it possible that she would have an extra day of liberty. However, we weren't sure how she would want to spend this time, which made packing a bit complicated.

It's nearly impossible to predict what a sailor will want to do during their liberty, and it's even more difficult when their time is restricted; planning for multiple outcomes is best. Some sailors want nothing more than peace, quiet, and some time with their family, to enjoy their freedom in a relaxed atmosphere where they can visit and catch up on things back home. So it's a good idea to pack clothes for that. Others want to be out and about and may have plans for visiting popular landmarks like Navy Pier, Millennium Park, or the Chicago Riverwalk. They might just want a fast-food hamburger, or a fine meal at a popular restaurant, or to gorge on greasy, buttery popcorn in a movie theater. We prepared for this by having the right clothes for the weather that were both casual enough for walking around but nice enough for slightly more formal settings.

We planned our trip so we would arrive the day before the ceremony and could allow for an extra day of liberty due to the holiday. This meant the first day for arrival and preparation, the second day for the ceremony, and a possible third day for liberty. On the fourth day, she was expected to leave for school, so we planned to say goodbye and, if possible, spend some time with her at the airport. The fifth day was our return trip home. We also prepared ourselves for the possibility that the holiday wouldn't affect her liberty at all, and we would need to fill a day without our sailor. (If the holiday hadn't fallen on the weekend, we would have planned the entire trip for four days instead of five.)

Each of us packed according to the weather forecast in the Chicago area and our own Floridian tolerance for cooler late fall weather. As for our sailor, we expected her to stay in uniform for most of her liberty, but we also thought there might be times when she would want to go back to our room at the Navy Lodge and rest; if so, she would likely want to change into comfortable civilian clothes.

Mom took care of packing for our sailor, including pajamas, lounging clothes, undergarments, and her favorite comfortable shoes. We packed an entire trip's worth of clothes just for her, even though we weren't sure if she would be able to wear any of them. Still, having those choices for her felt like the best option.

We also included her ukulele. Her true passion was her guitar, but we didn't want to risk losing or damaging something that expensive during the flight; we were traveling on a limited budget, and we didn't have much faith that her beloved instrument would be handled with care by the airlines we were using. In contrast, the ukulele could be kept with our personal items and carry-on bags, safely guarded by her loving and caring parents.

After all things were considered and planned for with the best of our (limited) experience, we could only wait. Each list was checked and revised, albeit only slightly. We packed everything for our sailor, as well as most of our own bags, the day before. Anything that we could store in our vehicle the night before, we did. We attempted to sleep.

The following morning commenced with breakfast, showers, getting dressed, and packing the toiletries we had used that morning into the last of the travel bags. We locked up the house, hopped into the car, and headed for the airport. Finally, after nearly three months of anxiety, stress, and uncertainty, we were on our way to Great Lakes to see our sailor.

04. Great Lakes

We arrived at O'Hare safely and without any delays. The airport was easy to navigate, but unlike our hometown airport, the rental car pickup was separate from the terminals. We took a short train ride to get there, but the signage wasn't helpful, and we had some trouble with our old, dilapidated bags. One of the heavier suitcases had no working wheels, so I had to awkwardly carry it through the airport. At one point, we decided to use a baggage trolley, only to find out that we were just an elevator ride away from the train platform. We had to abandon the trolley before boarding the train, but a nearby attendant assured us we could get another one once we arrived at our stop. Unfortunately, there weren't any to be found, and I had to lug the cumbersome suitcase through the garages and to the rental car desk.

We were glad we had ordered the toll transponder before the trip. If we hadn't brought our own, the rental car company could have provided one for a fee, in addition to the tolls. It turns out that the extra charges and fees would have far exceeded the cost of the $25 transponder and the toll charges we did end up paying. Thankfully, we could decline the added expense.

With keys in hand, we loaded up the rental car and set off for the roadways and vistas of this new, exotic land called Illinois.

This part of our trip didn't offer much for sightseeing, as the airport was located outside of the more densely packed streets of Chicago. The areas we did pass through weren't the crowded urban jungle we had imagined; in truth, it didn't feel too different from cities in Florida. These quickly gave way to open roads as we headed north toward

Great Lakes. I was thankful for this because we were ready to get to the hotel, drop off our bags, and prepare to see our sailor the next day. The last thing we wanted to deal with was city traffic.

Finding the Navy Lodge wasn't difficult. Upon arriving, we were informed that we needed to have our license plate number, IDs, and rental car agreements ready. I waited in the lobby as it slowly filled up with active-duty military and families, while my wife went back to the vehicle to take a picture of the license plate and grab the required documents. We wanted to check the accessibility of the room first, so we left most of our bags in the car, in case we needed to switch rooms or find another place entirely.

Our room was only a short distance down the hall from the lobby, conveniently located on the ground floor and close enough to the exits to make coming and going rather easy. As we passed the doors of other rooms, I saw that several of them were decorated with personalized anchors hanging from them. Each one was a unique creation that usually had a family name, ship number, and division painted, etched, or applied decoratively in some manner or other. A quick look down the hall revealed many more, and I suddenly felt like we had missed an opportunity to fully celebrate our sailor's accomplishment. With my mind racing to come up with some way to make up for this oversight, I unlocked the door with our key card.

The room was clean and comfortable, with two queen-sized beds and a bathroom that met Little Sister's accessibility needs. Considering the price and convenience, not to mention the general reputation of government-funded "perks", I had half expected stained linens or a strange smell. I had traveled on a budget for business and stayed at some questionable places. Once during my own tentative attempts to enlist, I was put up in a cheap motel during my medical processing. Both of those experiences set my expectations low. In fact, I was quite ready for a disappointing room and to hear complaints from my wife and daughter.

Those expectations were proven wrong. The room was better than expected, especially considering the price and the proximity to the base. I was pleasantly surprised, and so was the rest of the family. We took some time to settle in and unpack. That's when Mom pulled a thin cardboard box from her suitcase. She opened it to reveal a metal anchor, perfectly sized to hang on the door like the others I had seen. This one was jet black, with our name and sailor's information cut out of the metal. It was a beautifully crafted ornament. I looked at her, utterly surprised.

Mom had joined several social media groups, and they had mentioned these anchors. They were apparently such a common thing that the Navy Lodge keeps a box of door hangers available in the lobby for anchors. She had looked online and found someone on Etsy who made this for us. What amazed me was how beautiful it was in its minimalist design. It was perfectly suited for us and, more importantly, for our sailor.

She hung it on the door, smiling proudly.

We quickly finished our unpacking and assessed our time and preparations for the following days. We were still operating under the assumption that we would have a full day of liberty with her, due to the holiday; however, our ability to communicate with our sailor was limited. We had no idea what she would want to do with the rest of her day following PIR, or how we would spend an entire day of liberty the day after that.

It's easy to imagine the days leading up to a major graduation ceremony in the armed forces. An incredible amount of work goes into the final preparations. At the same time, the graduates also have to pack for departure for the next phase of their training. Additionally, the job of being a sailor didn't end. There were still physical training exercises and other duties that needed to be performed. All of this is packed in and around rehearsals for the event. For performance divisions, this also means additional practice.

For the graduates, PIR is an exhausting day. We weren't surprised to hear that many sailors choose to spend some of their liberty simply dressed in comfortable civilian clothes, sitting around, doing nothing, and indulging in the food and snacks they have been missing for ten or more weeks. With the comfortable clothing already secured (as I said earlier, we had already packed pajamas and lounging clothes in anticipation of this), we only had to stock up on some things we believed our sailor might want to eat.

We found ourselves at a nearby Super Target. Like other nationwide chains, we could reasonably expect things to be similar to our neighborhood stores, so it was easy to find what we needed at the price we expected. In addition to groceries, we could also grab any additional supplies we might have forgotten to pack.

We loaded the cart with all kinds of things. Our kids are generally good eaters, so junk food wasn't at the top of the list (but I made sure it was penciled in at the bottom). Little Sister and I grabbed some lesser essentials. The room had a coffee maker, so we picked up some dark roast, bottled water, and a few other things on Mom's list. We rounded out the cart with some personal preferences as well, including Reese's Cups, chips, and other guilty pleasures.

Meanwhile, Mom took care of the important things. Number one on the list was apples. Not just any apples, though—common Granny Smiths or Red Delicious were not on the menu. Mom knew that Gala apples were our sailor's favorite, so she went on a quest to find them. After an exhaustive search in the produce section, she came up empty-handed. She then found a night-time Target employee who also believed in the importance of finding the elusive (but very important) Gala apple.

They found four.

It's completely reasonable to think that we may have been budget-conscious in our purchases. After all, we were not flush with disposable income, and most of that trip added to our already sizable credit card debt. However, being overly cautious ran the risk of saying no to the wrong food items. We knew what our sailor liked, we just didn't know what she would want during liberty. And so we overspent, by any standards. Most of the food would probably go uneaten by us, but we felt the expense was justified. We could pass along the unopened food to the Navy Lodge staff or the next visitor to the room. But if we got it wrong, we weren't sure we would have the time to make another trip to the store, so we covered as many bases as we could.

There was a real chance that we were settling in for a family weekend in Chicago, while our sailor would not be able to be with us. There was also a very good chance she might choose to be somewhere else.

As parents, we tend to project our feelings. We believe that our separation from our kids is an emotional two-way street. We missed them, so they must have missed us just as much, maybe even more. Our own little cocktail of worry and separation anxiety makes us forget that we were once their age, and for many of us, we couldn't wait to get out from under our parents' shadow as soon as humanly possible. This was their time to leave the nest and embark on a brand new and exciting adventure. More importantly, they were isolated from us by design. They weren't just being trained; their dependence on us was being stripped away. The Navy showed them that they were capable, independent adults who could overcome obstacles, trials, and immense difficulty without their parents helping them or holding them up.

And without the safety net of their parents, they formed

other support systems and new relationships. These people were there with them when we were not, during this transformation from which we were rightly excluded. To this end, graduation doesn't just mean they become sailors; it also means they are moving on. The coming liberty would not only be a brief vacation from training, but also the last time they would see each other ever again. This was goodbye.

I knew there was a tomorrow after tomorrow for our family. We arrived in Illinois to celebrate the ceremony, but we also needed to be ready for our sailor to want to spend some time—a few hours, a few days, or her entire liberty—holding onto these new friendships without us getting in the way. There will be time enough in the future for us to be together; the same can't be said for these new relationships.

Mom, Little Sister, and I had to be prepared to spend our time without our sailor. We would still get our moment to embrace her, celebrate her, and love her at PIR. But she may have her own ideas on how to spend the time following the ceremony. We considered this time as our daughter's day, her time, and the best way to show our love was to keep our agendas and our hopes to ourselves, out of respect for her choices. We wanted her to choose without guilt, pressure, or any feeling of obligation to us. We hoped to celebrate this time together, but that did not constitute an agreement or debt to us that required payment from her. After all, the real reason we were in Great Lakes was to honor her achievement, not impose on her liberty.

It wasn't an easy truth to have to accept, and I dreaded the prospect that we might lose any time with her. But I had long ago learned that the greatest constant in being a parent is sacrifice.

05. Pass In Review

I am not a big fan of life hacks. In my experience, these unnecessary shortcuts are about as honest and effective as the concept of quality fast food. You don't tend to achieve your goals when you try to work around the standards, so if you want your food fast, you can expect the quality to suffer.

However, I am not against using tools. I frequently travel to destinations on familiar roads using my phone's map app to guide the way, despite my knowledge of the roads. I do this because the tool shows me traffic in real time, often letting me avoid delays caused by clever people ignoring their app and feeding traffic jams. So, when my wife presented an alternative route to the Pass in Review that she found on the internet—which effectively doubled the route my phone suggested we take—I was skeptical.

Being an experienced husband, I knew two things that would justify taking this longer route. The first element is that we had planned to leave early, and all things were in place to ensure this plan would work effectively enough, even with delays, so we should have plenty of time. Secondly, the inevitability of this taking longer meant I could deposit some I-told-you-so points in my dwindling account.

I agreed to the alternative route, under the condition we test drive it the night before. We did. For all intents and purposes, it would take twice as long to reach our destination, but I said nothing. We knew the route, we had the time, so we agreed to take it.

The next morning, we woke up, got ready, and headed out with only a few minor delays. We grabbed some portable food from the continental breakfast in the Navy Lodge's lobby, and the three of us hopped into the car. I pulled out my phone, opened the map app, punched in the address, and noticed with amused astonishment that the time it would take to reach the base had doubled overnight.

Both routes took around the same time, considering when we were departing. But those long lines on the direct route to the base would also become more congested the longer we were in them. Ultimately, the long way around was both easier and probably much faster than the shorter, direct way. My wife was even kind enough to agree that normally she wouldn't have put much stock in a route sourced from social media, but we were both glad she had learned about it.

I am not one to begrudge a good alternative when I'm proven wrong. I don't mind if the occasional life hack, workaround, or clever trick sometimes works. I lost my potential I-told-you-so points, and we took the long way around, bypassing the long lines through a less direct route.

We arrived at the gate and were pleasantly greeted by armed guards. Their friendliness contrasted with their dangerous appearance. I half-expected that the frustration of the car line would have seeped into their morning mood, but either we had arrived before it got out of hand or they were very practiced at ignoring such issues. We presented our tickets and IDs at the gate and were kindly directed to the garage. We parked easily and made our way inside, comfortably ahead of schedule.

The ceremony was in a long, hall-like building, with seating lined against the long side for guests. All the seats were grouped, with signage denoting where the different divisions would be standing during the event. Based on the layout and the directions provided by the sailors standing there to assist everyone, it was nearly impossible to be sitting in a place where the family wouldn't be able to enjoy a great view of their sailor standing proudly in formation.

We split up at this point. Little Sister and Mom got floor seats reserved for wheelchair accessibility. These seats were reserved so that one person in a wheelchair could be accompanied by a single guest. I made my way to the top of the bleachers, toward the back corner where the bleachers met the wall.

This seemed like it would be one of the more comfortable areas. Sure, it was higher up than most, but bleachers are uncomfortable in any environment, and being able to lean back against the wall was much kinder on my back. There is no benefit to sitting lower down on the bleachers in uncomfortable seats with no backs.

I later learned about an alternative to being cramped in a crowd of people: above the bleachers were balcony seats that were almost completely vacant. Had I known those seats were accessible to me, I could have been in the much less congested and more comfortable-looking balcony; they were still bleachers, but without the crowd of people it would have been much easier to stretch out and get comfortable.

At the time, I thought I had scored a really great seat. I leaned against the stone wall behind me and did my best to relax and enjoy the show.

The PIR ceremony is an impressive display of Navy pageantry. The bands play beautifully. Drill teams display an acrobatic exhibition of twirling, flipping, and tossing rifles. There are parades of impressive flags, marching, and award ceremonies, which should be expected in a military display. But there is more to the presentation: there's an emotional connection to everything about it, which is a unique experience for each person watching their loved one take part.

I watched my sailor move among a sea of impressively professional graduates. I was overflowing with pride and love. These were the heavy emotions I expected to have; what was unexpected and surprisingly all-encompassing was a sense of awe. At the core of this was how impressed I was with my sailor's accomplishment and her place in this living history. The institution of the United States Navy has existed since before the country won its independence. Before that stretches an even longer history of sailors and seamanship, dating back to the ancient world. This group of sailors represents the next iteration of that legacy. My child, my sailor, is now a part of this history.

Whenever I hear the words "navy" or "sailor" in any context, it now holds a different meaning. It isn't an abstract institution of boats and warfare at sea. It isn't an identity rooted in derivative ideas or understood through historical accounts or fictional representations. It now has an association for me that redefines what a sailor is and who they are. It has a connection to me that is real and informed through my relationship with a person who is now taking part in this tradition.

This was quite possibly an overblown sentiment from a generally romantic and imaginative mind with a nerd-like fascination for history. These unique impressions are mine because of my proclivities, and most people will bring their own biases and fascinations with them. Still, I think it is safe to say that the impression this event leaves on someone will be unique to each individual—but I don't think it will be any less profound.

It was one of those times where I ignored the impulse to take pictures or videos. I didn't want to experience this event through the viewfinder of a camera or by watching a small screen. Besides, it seemed foolish to do so when the entire event was already being documented in pictures and videos by the Navy.

More importantly, this was a singular event. I wouldn't get to see her graduate from boot camp ever again. This was the one chance I had to witness this accomplishment in person. I saw and heard the entire thing, and I remember it vividly. I'm glad the only pictures I took were the ones from directly after the event. And although we purchased the DVD created by the Navy videographers, I never watched it, and I can't think of a moment when I would. The event is captured forever in my memory, and I am glad I was an active witness to it.

And yet, I am ashamed to admit, as the event went on, a small part of me wished it would just end. After an hour, a seed of annoyance took root and began to grow. I was getting tired watching all the marching, saluting, flag-waving, horn-blowing, and general Navy-ing about. I watched people with impressive ribbons, medals, and ranks give speeches and receive justified honors. These were impressive people, whom I respected due entirely to their accomplishments and dedication to service to our country. I looked out into a hall filled with people who were committed to a higher ideal than I ever aspired to.

And I wished they would all just sit down, be quiet, and tell us we could go and hug our kids. Why did there have to be so much ceremony in this ceremony? My bottom was starting to hurt, and my mind began to wonder what we might be having for lunch after this.

As the event continued, I tried to imagine what the sailors standing statuesquely at attention were feeling. By that point, I could imagine the novelty of the occasion had worn off. I was sure the ten weeks or so of marching and standing during training had reduced the physical effort required to stand like this for so long. Yet they were moments away from being done with this part of their journey. Their families and loved ones, and some much-earned liberty, were very close, tantalizingly close. The only thing between them and a bit of their old life was a ceremony that seemed to want to drag on forever.

Regardless of how it might have felt at the time, the event wasn't excessively long. Not a moment of it was wasted on any kind of nonsense or filler. Every element honored or celebrated something important; there was no fat to trim. It was expertly organized and executed with rapid precision. There was just so much of it, and for the parents and loved ones who had been missing their sailor, it could easily feel like a roadblock between them and seeing this person they had been missing for months.

And then it was over. Abruptly, the entire event just ended, definitively. The solemnity was banished from the room in a flurry of sudden movement. Reverent silence was replaced by a cacophony of hollow thumping as shoes pounded down the bleachers. The waiting loved ones surged forward, dispensing with their restraint and self-control as though invisible leashes had been stretched until they snapped. Suddenly freed, they swarmed onto the floor toward the stoic line of sailors. The mass of uniformed men and women broke from their orderly ranks and moved like a tide toward the eager arms of loved ones as the two groups swirled together into crowds of hugs, kisses, and tears.

It was surprising how easily each sailor and family seemed to magnetically find each other through the islands of families and loved ones. These islands amassed into larger collections, and then they all seemed to drift apart, and the groups of people leaked out of the hall. It was slow and almost imperceptible, but soon the place was a large empty hall with only small groups scattered throughout.

Mom received the first hug, and Little Sister joined in. I observed as their arms enveloped and almost swallowed up our sailor, their faces buried in the embrace. It was a beautiful and magical moment, brimming with so much love, that I felt like an outsider. I didn't dare interrupt; it seemed almost irreverent to disturb such a moment. I knew my own turn to be a part of this would come soon enough, but right then, I was meant to be a witness and remain physically disconnected from it. Even in watching from the outside, I still felt the full weight of that love. It was a strange vantage point—connected only tangentially, while also being utterly a part of it.

After the hugs and praises, our sailor led us around the room and introduced us to other graduates and friends she had trained with, as well as the sailors and Recruit Division Commanders (RDCs) who had helped her succeed at boot camp. We moved around the small islands of families still lingering in the hall, searching for everyone who had aided her so she could proudly introduce them to her family. She wanted us to meet the people who had helped her achieve this pivotal moment of success.

Every single sailor we met was glowing with earned pride. Every smile was enormous and filled with unrelenting enthusiasm, their eyes shining and their energy bubbling. It was a day of a thousand accomplishments.

Eventually, we were asked to move along; our sailor had to report back to her ship (the training building, not an actual ship). We agreed to meet up at the NEX. After more hugs, words of pride, "good job"s, and "I love you"s, we went our separate ways.

The NEX and other buildings were popular places for families to regroup. The outside was packed, with groups of civilians milling around as they waited for their sailors. We went inside to do some shopping. We picked up a few Navy Dad and Navy Mom shirts and hoodies; there was quite a collection of items, and we had trouble narrowing down our choices to just a few affordable things.

It took some time before our sailor returned. We had finished shopping for ourselves long before, but she had a few more things to grab on the way out. This was an excellent opportunity to find out more about life on base. I was definitely curious, but even if I had been eager to leave, I would have asked her to show us around. She had been gone for over two months, and I felt the best way I could show my support was by expressing my interest in what life had been like for her here.

Unfortunately, the base was largely closed to civilians, and we could only explore the ceremony hall and the NEX. Still, we got a peek at the area where they made phone calls: it was a rather depressing little room, with payphone-like terminals. She also showed us the area where they did their shopping, which was separated from the NEX (which non-recruits get to enjoy).

Their shopping area was completely different, and unexpectedly so. There were markings on the floor designating a footpath, guiding you as to how you were supposed to move through the store. I found it amusing to think of myself in a line with other sailors, walking this preset path and grabbing things from the shelves as I passed by. It seemed perfectly reasonable and utterly alien at the same time. I couldn't help but wish, a little bit, that this was how grocery stores worked in the civilian world. How much nicer would it be if I didn't have to maneuver a shopping cart past someone standing in the middle of the aisle, obliviously reading the label of a can of peas and blocking the way for everyone else?

I found two aspects to be wonderfully helpful in explaining the day-to-day life of being in boot camp: order and restriction. Aside from the grueling training, tests, classes, and marching, actual living is a part of life on base. The rigidity of something as seemingly innocuous as shopping for hygiene products and other essentials drove home how different life must be in this isolated world.

On the one hand, I feel like having this kind of regimental order can be helpful in maintaining a sense of security. On the other hand, it is also very unlike the outside world, and losing the kind of freedom we usually take for granted must be difficult. While it may have been surprising to be restricted and have everything specifically defined and regulated, I wonder if that same strictness made it easier to acclimate. But when I asked what this must have been like, the most profound description I got was a generic "It sucked."

There is probably a lot about life at boot camp that is nearly impossible to empathize with. There aren't any analogous experiences in civilian life. I can generally picture how difficult life at RTC might have been, but to truly understand it is impossible without having gone through it. Throughout the phone calls and conversations over the following days, we got a general list of grievances and complaints that painted an explicit picture of a life that generally fell into variations of "it sucked."

Despite this, I had never seen our sailor standing so strong and proud of who she had become. She was happy she had done this. There was something deep in this experience that she loved being a part of. And while there was quite a lot about boot camp she was glad to leave behind, there was clearly an element of it she had enjoyed.

It had also transformed her. She had become a stronger, more defined, and more confident version of herself. The core essence of the child I had known—who had grown up to be strong, vibrant, kind, intelligent, and full of love—was still there; not a single aspect of that person had been taken away. But the Navy had profoundly changed her. Boot camp had added something to her, or given her something more to become. She had gained new skills, of course, but that alone doesn't make you different in an existential sense. There was something deeper: a combination of purpose, pride, and confidence that came together and enhanced the essence of who she was.

She was still the person I had always known, loved, and respected. She was just more. And now, we would finally have the opportunity to spend some time getting to know this new, exciting individual.

06. Liberty

"Liberty" is used by the Navy in the same way civilians might say "time off work." I find the use of the word amusing. 'Liberty' is often defined as being free or no longer restricted or oppressed. When I consider some popular associations with liberty and what people have had to go through in the past to achieve the concept, it gets a little dark. But this is getting hung up on semantics—until we consider that the sailor's freedom after PIR is surprisingly limited. Those restrictions are merited, but they also define liberty very narrowly for the sailor: they are at liberty to leave the base, but they are not free from their responsibility to act and conduct themselves as sailors.

I don't disagree with these constraints. I understand them, and I would endorse these rules if the Navy had asked my opinion on the subject. Surprisingly, they didn't; if they had, I would have told them to keep the rules and enforce them to the extent that those in charge feel is warranted, but change the term. "Liberty" is a fun word to use in theory, but the way it is applied is not very honest, because there is a remarkable lack of freedom in this liberty.

When in public, the sailor must remain in uniform and up to Navy standards. This also means that while outside, they must wear their cover ('hat' to us civilians), and when indoors, their cover is removed. While inside a place available to the public, including the hallways or lobby of a hotel, they must remain in uniform, but while in the privacy of a home or a hotel room, they may dress in good old non-Navy-issued clothes. There are rules against drinking and smoking, how far they can travel, how they can travel, and what time they can leave the base and when they must return.

Luckily, the sailors know these rules, and they are in-centivized to respect them by the mere presence of other sailors and RDCs living their own lives around town. While some bending, breaking, or ignoring of these rules may seem simple, innocuous, or even inane, it is much easier to respect them than it is to defend the choice to defy them. Even worse is the possibility of a sailor having to face some consequence for failing to live up to their new responsibilities.

Liberty is not universally granted. Some sailors will not get any liberty, depending on their rate. After PIR, they will go immediately to "A" School nearby. Those who have to travel to "A" School may get the remainder of the day of the ceremony. For sailors who were heading to their "A" School by plane, there was an opportunity to visit with them at the airport while they waited for their departure. A rare and special few were lucky to get an additional day, for no other reason than that the calendar coincidentally put graduation day right before a holiday weekend.

Our first hours of her liberty were simple and ordinary. It was the middle of the day of the PIR ceremony, and we were able to gather our sailor shortly after the event and head off the base. We were hungry and looking for a place to eat. We wanted something unique to the area but still familiar and comforting—something like home but not something available in Florida. Eventually, we settled on an absurd combination of wonderful comfort food at a place called Create Your Own Cheesecake & Cheesesteak. The restaurant had a very basic cafeteria aesthetic—simple, clean, but old and in need of repair. The slightly neglected interior stood in stark contrast to the quality of the food, as is often the case in such places. The cheesesteak was won-derful, and the cheesecake was a great follow-up. I think we all enjoyed our food there. But it turned out that we weren't the only ones who thought the place offered a good lunch.

One piece of sage advice given to me long ago by an old roommate, whose profession was best described as 'aspiring punk-rock guitarist', was to eat where the EMTs, firefighters, and police eat. If it's lunchtime and there are a bunch of uniforms eating there, you can be assured the food is good, regardless of the establishment's appearance. To this day, that advice has held up: if a place looks new and untried but there are cops parked outside, it's probably a good place to eat. I imagine this also holds true for military personnel near a base.

Not long after we sat down to enjoy our sandwiches, two men in Navy uniforms entered the restaurant. They noticed our sailor and pleasantly greeted and congratulated her. Then they jokingly warned her to keep quiet and not pollute their favorite places to eat with recruits. It was a short, friendly exchange, and an overall pleasant surprise.

This encounter reinforced the need to respect the rules for liberty. We hadn't been off the base for an hour before eyes and ears from the Navy showed up where we were having lunch. And why not? This is their home during their posting here, and I imagine there are a ton of people working at RTC who also pop in and out of places during their daily lives. The last thing a graduate wants to experience during their break is a reprimand because they couldn't follow simple rules after having regulations drilled into them for at least two and a half months.

After lunch, our sailor just wanted to relax. This was one of the options we had planned for. I don't know if the extended leave granted by the holiday would have changed it; it was pretty evident she was tired. I think we all had enough energy to do a bit of sightseeing if she preferred, but since we were given the extra day, we took advantage of it and headed back to our room at the Navy Lodge.

Mom's clever planning won the day. She had packed the

correct clothes and shoes, and of the food we purchased the night before, the apples were a big hit. We lounged around, half-watched a movie on TV, snacked, and drank an absurd amount of coffee. We may have opened half of the abundance of groceries. I set aside everything else that had been unopened, to leave it for the staff.

It was a wonderfully lazy afternoon. Our sailor took a long shower, relishing the slower pace. No one was barking orders. No one was tapping a clock and rushing people along. Here, she could do something that was never a part of boot camp: she could waste time, she could relax.

This was also our best time to get the unvarnished truth of how training really went for her. She was open to our questions, and she was able to be honest and unfiltered. There were no other recruits nearby on phone calls who might catch a stray word or phrase and get the wrong idea. There were no RDCs watching. There was unlikely to be anyone listening in through the phones for anyone giving away secrets. Essentially, there was no reason not to be honest.

The truth was far less frightening than we had expected. Our sailor was very happy to discuss her training. There were, of course, some things that she kept secret, but she spoke excitedly of her experience. She told stories of learning to put out fires, how her sinus cold may have helped her tolerate the infamous Confidence Chamber, how nervous she was for the final test (Battle Stations), and how exhilarating the entire experience had been. It sounded like the most difficult thing she had ever experienced in her relatively short life up to that point, but she seemed to really love it.

There were other elements that seemed to bleed over from civilian life into boot camp. Social structures formed and needed to be navigated, which was made more difficult by her appointment as a Starboard Watch Section Leader.

Boot camp was clearly a time for professional, physical, and emotional evolution.

As the discussion wore on, and the breaks between questions lengthened as we struggled to find gaps in our knowledge that needed filling, I saw the growth manifested in this person. I wasn't learning about her experience at boot camp: I was learning more about *her*. I was watching this strong person who embraced difficult trials, faced fear, and navigated challenges as she told her stories with a broad smile and excitement beaming in her eyes. She may have been exhausted, but she seemed able to talk about her new life for hours.

My own concerns seemed to wash away with this casual interrogation. She had made the right choice. She was a sailor. And over the next couple of days, I would learn so much more about what being a sailor meant for her and how it would affect our family.

Despite the languid pace of the hours, the day eventually came to an end. We ordered dinner from a local restaurant, and had it delivered to the room, where it arrived cold and incomplete. Out of time, we were forced to accept the quality and eat what we had gotten. Afterward, our sailor abandoned the comfort of her civilian loungewear and got dressed back in uniform.

We had no way to gauge how traffic at the base was going to be, so we left thirty minutes earlier than we needed to for the ten-minute drive. It turned out to be warranted, as we were in line at the gate for an extra ten minutes. Once we passed the guard station, we parked in the lot beside the NEX.

We only had a few minutes for hugs and goodbyes. It wasn't as difficult this time; there wasn't a ten-week gap of unknowns approaching us. There was still one more day of liberty, and there might be an opportunity to see her at the airport before her departure for "A" School.

She fell in with a group of friends, and we watched the sailors walk back into the secret places of the base where we are not permitted to enter. Exhausted but excited for the next day and our adventures in Chicago, we left the base and returned to the hotel. But on that silent trip back, there was a very obvious absence. Once again, there were only three of us, and it felt like there should have been four.

07. Chicago

We woke up early and quickly got dressed. I used the small drip coffee maker in the room to make some liquid fuel, and we hurried out. On our way to the car, I stopped by the lobby and grabbed some individually wrapped pastries. They weren't the best breakfast option, but they were convenient and would hold us over for now. We needed to get to the base quickly to pick up our sailor; we would find a better source for breakfast later.

Outside, the fall weather hadn't fully transitioned to winter, but for three people used to Florida's definition of cold, it was bitterly uncomfortable. I expected it to warm up later, but in the early morning, before the sun had fully risen, the air still held the bite of night. Our short walk to the car from the hotel lobby felt like miles in a frozen wasteland.

The wet wind lashed around us, almost mischievously. Small gusts snuck up gently before suddenly snapping harshly, making us shiver and huddle together as if we were being attacked by little frost devils who retreated after stinging, letting us relax into a false sense of security before repeating the assault again and again. Mom and Little Sister mumbled complaints while wrapping their coats tighter. Once inside the car, Mom started the engine and began warming up, while I remained outside to load the wheelchair. By the time I finished, I regretted ever leaving the lobby.

Inside the car, I discovered the true appeal of seat warmers. In Florida, it never gets cold enough for an extended period of time for me to see the need for luxuries like seat and steering wheel warmers. But when I sat down on the cold seat, feeling the chill that had seeped into my jeans pressing against my legs, I became an enthusiastic fan of the electric miracle of seat warmers. My wife wrapped her hands around the warm steering wheel and sat there for a few moments, greedily absorbing the heat radiating from the wheel into her thawing palms and fingers.

If anyone had seen us sitting there, they would have thought that discovering modern climate control in a vehicle was the most important thing in the world that day. I wouldn't have blamed them for thinking we were barbarians, so utterly distracted by the mundane that we had forgotten about the real reason we woke up before the sun could properly dispel the chill. And as we giggled and marveled at this small luxury, it added to our already elevated spirits.

Today was going to be a second day of liberty with our sailor. It was a rare and wonderful treat for most graduates and their families, and we intended to make the most of it. Since the holiday weekend delayed the flight to "A" School, we had the day to rest and relax after the ceremony, followed by an additional day for adventures in the city.

Over dinner the previous evening, we had discussed ideas for how to spend the time, worried that our sailor might want to spend it without us. Luckily, she had a list of sights she wanted to see in Chicago (starting with the Navy Pier), and she wanted to experience it with her family. But before that, we had to pick her up from the base and address the first item on our collective list: a proper sit-down breakfast.

The security gate at the base was less busy this time. This was partly due to the more sporadic and less defined departure times. Not as many people had liberty, and some families couldn't stay the extra day, and those who did spend the day with their sailors arrived at random times. We quickly passed through security and pulled up to the NEX parking lot, which had become the default drop-off and pickup point for most families.

Seeing her standing tall and proud in the uniform she had earned was still surprising. I towered over her as I stood beside her, and I still felt like I was looking up to her. For the rest of the day, I was standing in her shadow, grinning like an idiot.

We headed south toward Chicago to visit Navy Pier. The drive would take us close to an hour, so we decided to stop for an early breakfast in the nearby town of Lake Forest at a place called Egg Harbor Café. I'm a sucker for country-style breakfast food like biscuits with gravy and omelets, and Egg Harbor Café was the perfect place for us. The food was fantastic, and the setting and staff were welcoming and friendly. We ended up ordering more food than we intended, but we ate most of it and left the table feeling pleasantly full. Of all the places we visited in the Chicagoland area, the Egg Harbor Café was by far my favorite place to eat.

With breakfast happily settled, we headed to Navy Pier. We planned to spend most of our time in the city on foot rather than in the car, so we found parking in a garage about a mile away from the pier and abandoned our comfortable, electrically-warmed seats for the windy Chicago morning. Fortunately, the walk from the car to the pier was pleasant; the biting cold of the early morning had mellowed into a nice chill thanks to the morning sun.

The pier, however, resisted the warming trend, cooling the milder temperature with a damp breeze blowing in from Lake Michigan. It was only slightly more uncomfortable, but it had that typical gray and gloomy feel of a northern harbor—quiet, empty, and lonely. The few people wandering the pier seemed like trespassers in an abandoned idea.

It may have been the off-season, or the weather, but the emptiness was unexpected. Some music played from outdoor speakers, but the seagulls and other birds who hadn't migrated to warmer climates were much noisier. The wind whistled in our ears, and we walked mostly in silence, enjoying each other's company without needing to say a word.

Eventually, as if our presence had somehow given permission to others, people began to wander in. Soon, we saw other graduates and their families among the new arrivals walking the pier. They were easy to spot in their perfectly pressed uniforms, their backs straight and rigid as they walked with firm and deliberate steps. The afterglow of pride and accomplishment shone vibrantly on faces now learning how to settle back into a softer and more casual world. But relaxing into normalcy seemed to be fighting against an urge to maintain the stoic rigidity they had needed to uphold for the past ten weeks. Some even looked slightly awkward being out in the world again.

Our sailor decided to join with a friend from boot camp and her family, who were going to be in the area. For us, it seemed like a great opportunity to meet some of the people who were such a big part of her journey. It got Mom and I talking about how some of the other sailors had planned to get together with their friends to catch a movie, and how some of their families might not be too happy with the idea.

We can't deny we would feel some disappointment if our sailor wanted to spend her liberty watching a movie with a group of sailors. She had been living with them for ten weeks, while we had spent those weeks missing her and looking forward to seeing her again. Wouldn't we be frustrated at being cast aside for a movie?

But during those ten weeks, we civilians were able to watch movies, relax in front of a TV, and spend time with friends we could reasonably expect to see the next day, week, month, or even years later. Our sailors spent those ten weeks constrained to the base, living under a rigid set of

rules in a life regimented by daily schedules and training focused entirely on becoming sailors. During this time, they
bonded with other recruits. There were no movies, no TV
shows, and these final few days would very likely be the last
days they would see each other.

I never served. I can't begin to identify with the fear, the
challenges, and the pain our sailors go through in boot
camp. I can't imagine how important the bonds formed in
this shared experience might be. I can only understand, on
a basic level, what friendships look like when they are an
element pushing recruits past their own fears and limits, to
overcome and finally succeed. To have gone through all
that, only to celebrate success with a goodbye that very well
might mean forever, is a difficult thing to comprehend.

Looking back on it, I am astonished at how casually the
graduates seemed to understand and accept this. They were
saying goodbye to these relationships casually, oblivious to
their impermanence. The inevitability of this separation—
that their lives and futures would soon take them on paths
that diverged ever wider and were unlikely to cross again—
must have hung heavily over them. But they were still young
and behaving as young people do, with the sureness that
these connections were perpetual, unending. They were
hanging out, carrying on, enjoying each other's company,
having fun, and living in these moments regardless of their
ephemerality, convinced that these bonds would last forever.

Maybe, in some way, they will.

We connected with our daughter's friend and her family. Soon, the two sailors were walking ahead of us. Both
families seemed to know, without saying anything, that we
should allow space for them, just the two of them. They
walked together, talking and laughing, having their own moment on the pier while their families followed, partial participants enjoying their company from a short distance.

I loved it. We were still part of the experience with our sailors, while getting a peek into this new world that was entirely theirs. They had a language unto themselves—their jokes and stories, which would cause incomprehensible laughter in the two of them, were unintentionally private.

It was reassuring when I realized how much of this I needed to see. It was suddenly in front of me: she was owning this new life and the future it was offering. This was hers now, stepping out from under the sheltering shadow of her parents and having an identity independent of her family. She was a person fully independent of being my child. She had grown up.

This wasn't an epiphany. I didn't stand there dumbfounded as some inner crescendo played in my head like an imaginary movie soundtrack. I knew, on some elemental and primal level, there was a change happening. I just wasn't mentally articulating it at the time. It is only by looking back that I can point to the moment when I saw it for the first time. The only thing I was aware of in my internal emotional soup in those moments was a steadily growing feeling of enjoyment and pride. It felt good and right to be there, witnessing this evolution—or rather, the aftereffects of an evolution she had undertaken during her training. There was a new sense of safety—a validation that it was okay for me to have let her go off on this adventure. It had worked out. She was strong enough to do this, and she had done it.

Finally, I could let go of the nagging fear that I had made a terrible mistake. I watched her with her people, with other sailors, in this new life of hers, and she was genuinely happy.

When we reached the end of the pier, we merged back into a single group. We spent some time there, idly enjoying the morning, and after taking some pictures, we headed into the central building. This is where the open shops and restaurants hide themselves after the summer season moves on and good sense means the outside stalls and tours have no business trying to wring a few final dollars out of tourists. We wandered around for about an hour, picking up some souvenirs and browsing the shops and stalls. Then we parted ways with the other sailor and her family to go on our separate adventures in the city.

We left the pier and ventured into the streets of Chicago, surrounded by towering buildings that cast shadows over the windy corridors they created. After discussing our options, we decided to go to the Starbucks Reserve Roastery for coffee and snacks instead of heading straight to Willis Tower (formerly the Sears Tower and the tallest building in Chicago). If our visit didn't take too long, we would have had time to see both, but the one with a wide variety of coffee and chocolate seemed more appealing.

Although we had some trouble with the route due to the wheelchair, it was a pleasant walk through the city. In spite of the occasional chills from random gusts of wind, the streets were bustling with people. After navigating through the midday crowds, a few wrong turns, and a shortcut through a hotel lobby, we found ourselves in the shadow of the roastery, a distinctive five story building on the corner of Erie Street and Michigan Avenue.

The first floor focused on coffee, offering the same Starbucks experience you can find anywhere—complete with strong aromatic enticements, long lines, and a disappointing attention to name pronunciation. A short flight of stairs (or in our case, an elevator ride) took us to the second floor, which housed a bakery. On the third floor, there were artisanal coffees with different flavor explorations that were too adventurous for me at the time but excited Mom and our sailor. The fourth floor featured a coffee-themed cocktail bar and brewery, which would have been more enticing later in the day if we had time. Finally, on the fifth floor, we found a small rooftop terrace, with a view of Michigan

Avenue and a skylight view into the roastery below.

Despite the roastery's large size, it was incredibly crowded. Little Sister and I headed to the terrace, grabbed some seats, and waited for Mom and our sailor to explore the other floors for food and drink. They took a long time to get through it all, so when they finally arrived, the coffee was tepid but still tasty. Thankfully, the pastries and baked goods were warm and much more enjoyable. However, the delays from waiting in the various lines took longer than we had expected. By the time we finished our food and drinks, the afternoon was waning, and we wanted to make at least one more stop before we ended the day.

For our final excursion, we decided to skip a trip to Willis Tower in favor of Millennium Park to see "The Bean" (or more formally, Cloud Gate). We headed to the garage to pick up the car and drove into the city. We found another garage under the park and took an elevator to a small enclosure at street level, next to a flight of stairs that led up to the entrance. The location was probably convenient for most people, but not for Little Sister's wheelchair, so we went searching and found an accessible ramp nearby that took us into the park at Lurie Garden.

The late fall weather wasn't kind to the garden. Its scope was impressive, but the mostly brown and dried-out plants were a stark contrast to the nearby pictures advertising its spring and summer beauty. Still, I could imagine how impressive it must be in the right season, and I hoped to revisit it in the summer to see the architect and the gardeners' ambitious vision properly realized.

The garden and the park were not the reason we had gone there: we had only been expecting to see The Bean. It hadn't occurred to us that it might reside in a park with its own impressive reputation and other attractions worth visiting, so the garden, even in its late-season decline, was an exciting bonus. A glance at a nearby map showed that there were more experiences worth investigating after The Bean, and I hoped to see as many as we could.

The day was quickly fading, so we headed straight to our primary goal. It didn't take long, and it didn't disappoint.

Cloud Gate is a triumph of vision and design. A colossal structure, it gleams with a seamless metallic surface that mirrors the vibrant blue sky, distorting the images of passing clouds and the surrounding Chicago skyline. The reflections were pulled, stretched, and warped by its amorphous body. As I approached, I could see it deforming my own image in a wonderfully disorienting way. I felt I could, maybe even should, walk up to it and into it. Its mercurial appearance defied its solidity, as if I could step through my own distorted reflection and into a nebulous otherworld beyond.

We walked around and under the sculpture, watching as our reflected images shifted and altered, changing in an almost expected but never predictable way. Underneath, in the center, is a concave shape called the omphalos, or navel, which transforms one's reflection into a swirling fluid. Reluctantly, I tore myself away from the transmuted imagery and continued my tour of the outside.

I found our sailor staring transfixed with a gaping child-like smile, her eyes round, her face beaming with an excited light. She and I share an admiration for art and science, but there is a special enthusiasm for the confluences of the two that redefine and transcend both. Here she was, gawking unapologetically with wild fascination at something that beautifully encapsulated this union. It was a joy only expressible by the young and adventurous, who can see so much wonder in things that are wonderful.

Eventually, we left The Bean and walked a short way to the Jay Pritzker Pavilion, a bandshell theater with outdoor seating that is home to the Grant Park Symphony Orchestra. There were no shows playing at the time, but we wanted to escape the crowds for a little while as we planned our next destination. The day was coming to an end, with the sun slowly setting behind the towering skyscrapers.

Our final stop was the Crown Fountain, which consists of a pair of fifty-foot-tall LED screens facing each other across a shallow reflecting pool. These screens display the faces of random Chicago residents, with water squirting out from the screens near the mouths of the faces to create the fountains. Unfortunately, the water wasn't flowing while we were there, as it is only active from May to October, but the structures themselves were nevertheless impressive. However, I couldn't quite grasp the aesthetic appeal of fifty-foot faces spitting water at me.

It did serve as another reminder that Millennium Park must be wonderful in the spring and summer. Nearing the end of autumn, we were witnessing a great attraction that had faded. Yet even at this less-than-ideal time of year, the park was still a thoroughly enjoyable experience. The Bean was the highlight of our visit, but I could envision the beauty that awaited in the garden, along the paths and walkways, with children playing in the reflecting pool between the Crown Fountain towers and a warm sun shining down. I hope to visit again—preferably in the spring, to witness the park in all its splendor.

Our day spent walking the pier, exploring the streets of Chicago, enjoying coffee at a massive Starbucks, and discovering the sights of Millennium Park was the kind of day that we could all appreciate. Each element offered something for each of us to enjoy. More importantly, it was a day centered around what our sailor wanted to see and do. For our part, we simply needed to find aspects of each experience that resonated with us.

If our sailor had had no interest in any of this, or she wanted to spend time with her friends instead, we would have had to accept our disappointment and respect her wishes. After all, her time was strictly limited by the Navy and her departure the following day. The rest of us weren't bound by such restrictions; our nights ended when we wanted them to, and our trip lasted as long as we had planned. If there was anything else we wanted to see or do, it had to be done outside of the time allocated to her by the Navy.

In the end, being open to what she wanted allowed us to be there with her on her terms. Ultimately, we had a wonderful experience. Furthermore, there was still another opportunity to enjoy some time with her, which gave us a surprising but interesting look inside her new world.

08. Shipping Out

When my wife woke me up the next morning, it was still dark outside. There was no sign of the usual predawn light that often precedes the early hours of the morning. It was pitch black, impenetrable, deep, and cold. If dawn was coming, it seemed to be hours away. For all I knew, I had only slept for an hour.

"We have to go," my wife said, speaking quietly. Not a whisper, more like the voice of someone who wanted to be gentle so as not to startle me. Still, her low, hushed tone was stern and deliberate, warding off any potential questioning or arguments. She wasn't informing me, she was commanding me, ordering me to get up and move.

It only took me a few moments to fully wake up, but it was a roller coaster of seconds. I didn't need an explanation for being woken up—all that mattered was that someone needed me, and I could gather information and think later. I got to my feet and started getting dressed. I had the sense that this was an emergency. I had to hurry. I was afraid something had gone horribly wrong. Parents often hear stories of attacks, suicides, and other frightening things. My imagination was working overtime to fit these horrors into the blank space after "we need to go", the implied "because..."

It only takes seconds for these thoughts to invade the foggy places in our brains that remain as we are waking up. All the concerns, doubts, and fears I typically ignored were screaming at me, slamming into me like a bus. Suddenly, every unlikely thing that could have gone wrong was happening all at once. It's irrational, and not even statistically likely, but somehow it was the only possible reaction for my sleep-addled brain. Within a few moments, I had gone from fully asleep to panicking at imaginary fears.

I was moving quickly, deliberately, but waiting for more information, any information, with which I could plan my next actions. As she woke Little Sister, my wife began explaining things. The fog in my head thinned and dissipated. The dark, shadowy fears were banished. As my wife relayed the series of events leading to our impending departure, the mundane reality of the situation settled in.

It was a little before 5:00 in the morning. My wife had hardly slept at all; instead, she had been texting with our sailor, trying to get information on the Navy's departure schedules for the graduates flying to "A" School. We had heard that it was possible to spend time at the airport with our sailor as she waited for her flight, but the details on how it would work were unclear. She couldn't get any definitive confirmation on when they would be heading out.

Then our sailor had sent a message. Buses had arrived at the base to pick up all of the sailors who had flights that day. She was able to confirm that we could meet her at the airport, but we didn't know how we would do this. We had said our goodbyes the day before, but any extra time spent together was worth trying for. With no other information, we gathered our things and headed for the car.

We went straight to the airport without making any stops. Mom spent the drive checking social media for any clues on where we should go to meet the sailors. The information was vague and nearly useless; the most we could gather was to head for Terminal 2. After looking at the airport map, this was an obvious choice: Terminals 1, 2, and 3 were within walking distance of each other and had the best access to most of the departing flights. There is no Terminal 4 at O'Hare, and Terminal 5 was more isolated from the other terminals.

While Terminal 2 seemed like the best option, we didn't

have a timetable or any concrete information on what to look for, and we weren't getting responses from our sailor. In our minds, our opportunity to see her was slipping away. Terminal 2 might be a good place to start due to its central location, but this was a huge international airport that we would have to cover. We needed information, and we needed to hurry.

In order to spend the day with her, we needed to meet up with her while she checked in, so we could get a visitor pass that would allow us through security. She wouldn't be able to wait for us—if her check-in happened before we could find her, we would miss our opportunity, and last night's goodbye would have been the end of our visit with her in Illinois.

We attempted to fill in the information gaps ourselves, but our plan was so flawed that it should never have worked: essentially, all it involved was parking and looking around. The only things that were really in our favor were factors we hadn't considered, which were completely unknown to us then and beyond our control. So, our lack of knowledge only added to our stress, making us worry that we were losing our chance.

We decided to split up. Mom dropped off Little Sister and me at Terminal 2, while she went to park the car; we would meet up later. Little Sister and I rushed into the terminal and found it crowded, with people milling about. We thought it would be easy to spot a large group of uniformed Navy personnel, but even this distinction could get lost in the sea of travelers. It never occurred to us that the buses might not have arrived yet and we were looking for people who weren't even there.

We searched every corner of the terminal, maneuvering through groups of travelers idling, those waiting in line, and other people hurrying along the same paths we were taking. We approached airport staff who weren't busy with other travelers, hoping they could help. I was surprised to find that no one knew what I was looking for. I thought this would be a regular occurrence, with graduates frequently arriving in large groups to fly out, but the staff seemed completely unaware of such an event.

Throughout our search, we had sporadic contact with Mom. The cell reception inside the terminal was unreliable at best, and trying to reconnect with her while she also searched for the sailors made it even more difficult for us to find each other. Eventually, we finally regrouped, found our sailor, and realized how utterly ridiculous the past forty-five minutes had been.

I want to blame our lack of sleep, but it was really just a severe case of FOMO (fear of missing out). If we had taken even a few minutes to think things through, it would have been much easier for us. We could have started the day with a proper cup of coffee and some food, and we could have taken our time. We would have been able to focus without feeling rushed. But the fear of missing an extra day had us running aimlessly around, frantically searching for the sailors instead of assessing the situation. While waiting for our sailor to go through the check-in line, I had plenty of time to reflect on the stupidity of our morning.

The Navy graduates approximately 30–40,000 sailors a year in weekly PIR ceremonies. Even during times of low recruitment, we're still talking an average of about seven hundred sailors per week. Even considering that some of them go to "A" School in Great Lakes and only a fraction of the sailors depart from the airport, we're still dealing with a few hundred sailors in multiple buses.

If we had known better, we could have prepared better. The day before departure, we would have set up a messaging system—ideally, a group text. All of us would agree that any message or update would require a confirmation reply; otherwise, our sailor should assume we didn't receive the message and send another one every few minutes until she received a response.

Mom, Little Sister, and I would have planned to wake up at 5 AM. This isn't an unreasonable time to get ready; it's probably earlier than necessary, but it would make it much less likely for us to miss the text message, and we could be prepared to leave for the airport without feeling rushed. If we were lucky, we might have even been caffeinated.

Hundreds of sailors fly to different training bases for "A" School, with these flights taken through various commercial airlines. The Navy has become efficient at processing these departures, but it still requires organization and time. The first step for the sailors is to get loaded onto the buses. It takes time for the hundreds of sailors and their luggage to be ready. At this point, the sailors should be able to send a text indicating that they would be leaving, since during the bus trip, it's unlikely that the sailors would be able to contact anyone from their phones.

After receiving the message about the bus, Mom, Little Sister, and I would head to the airport and park at Terminal 2. There is no need to split up, as it would only complicate things. Terminal 2 is the most centralized location, and accessing the other terminals was easy to do from there. Also, the Bus/Shuttle Center is located there, on Level 1 of the main parking area in front of the terminal. Furthermore, it is unlikely that the buses would be able to load, travel, arrive, and unload in the same time it would take us to make the drive and park.

Once at the airport, the sailors are gathered in a central area, away from the general airport traffic. There are small sections between terminals that are perfect for this purpose. This is the most likely opportunity for them to use their phones again. They wait there for further instructions. That's where we found them, a large collection of sailors sitting near their luggage. After that, it's a waiting game. The sailors milled around, mostly in small groups, but they were generally quiet and alert as they waited for instructions. Eventually, they are handed their orders before proceeding to the ticketing area, where they line up to check in.

This was a crucial time: we had to be with her at this point to obtain our visitor pass into the airport. However, the line was very long, with hundreds of sailors waiting with their orders, luggage, and paperwork in hand. If we had not connected with the sailor by now, it would have been pretty easy for her to provide their location. A simple text could include the terminal, floor number (departing flights are on the ground floor), and any other identifiers: "Terminal 2, left side by the big yellow number 3 on the wall, bring coffee."

From this point on, it was simply a matter of finding our sailor among the hundreds milling around and standing in line. Once we found her, we waited in line together as a family until the sailor had checked in and we had our guest passes.

The entire process went smoothly and fluidly. Once she was checked in and all boarding and guest passes were acquired, we went through the TSA security checkpoint to get inside the airport. Depending on when the flight leaves, there might be a wait of several hours before the sailor is ready for boarding, or a frantic dash to the departure gate. In our case, our sailor wasn't scheduled to be at her gate until early evening, which meant a whole day of waiting.

O'Hare is a well-equipped and easily navigable airport, filled with shops, cafes, and restaurants. Groups of sailors waiting for their flights gather, play games, and socialize with each other. There is plenty to do there, but the cost and effort can be prohibitive.

We had planned for a day at the airport in our budget, which included dining there. However, money was not the only obstacle: guests are subject to the same security requirements as travelers, so we were limited in the supplies, water, food, and medications we could bring inside.

Additionally, there is a lot of walking involved on such a day, especially for sailors who want to say goodbye to friends departing from different terminals. With this in mind, we packed lightly, but it was still challenging to carry the few things we did bring back and forth through the airport. Accessibility, mobility, finances, and other restrictions can contribute to the stress and fatigue experienced when spending time in the airport.

The sailors might want some freedom to move around the airport, especially if they have a long wait. It would not be fair to our sailor if we were unable to keep up with her or if we caused her to miss opportunities to be with her friends. By deciding to be there, we were committing to being available to her on her terms; this meant that we would be there to spend time with her, but we would not get in her way if she wanted to be with her friends.

I thought long and hard about my ability to meet these standards. I was still recovering from a leg injury I sustained in a vehicle accident, and I was unsure if I could handle long hours of standing and walking. I was sore, and my leg was weak from the excessive walking the previous day. I agreed to the plan only on the condition that if I needed to rest, I would find a place to sit while the family continued without me, and I would catch up when I was able to.

I really wanted to be there. I wanted more time—any time—to spend with our sailor. I was not ready for this adventure to be over. And while spending a day at an airport with a group of graduating sailors may not win any "best of trip" awards, I found it to be one of the most rewarding aspects of our weekend.

09. Talk Like a Sailor

During our extended liberty in Chicago, we had the opportunity to spend time with other sailors. These encounters were usually brief and involved other family members and friends. Initially, I believed that we were seeing sailors who had transformed from their civilian identities, and in a sense, this was true. However, the graduates—including our own—were filtering their behavior, presenting a version of themselves that aligned more closely with their previous lives—still themselves, but in a censored manner. It was not until we spent time with them at the airport that we witnessed the more complete version of them.

The transformation that can occur in just ten weeks is remarkable. We observed their confidence and self-assurance, noticing how they carried themselves differently and how effortlessly they embodied the polished and disciplined demeanor of a sailor. However, when they gathered together in small groups (even as few as six), we witnessed an even greater shift. In the comfort of their camaraderie, bolstered by their familiarity with each other, and perhaps influenced by their uniforms and their uniformity, they began to revert back to their sailor selves. And sailors talk like, well, sailors.

I am not bothered by what some might consider "bad language." I find all forms of language usage interesting; whether it's foul language or accepted standards, or even invented language, it all fascinates me. I am intrigued when each new generation finds novel ways to manipulate and redefine words, as if creating a secret code to confound previous generations. Words are a form of expression, and how they are used can give them context or infuse them with greater meaning. Their application can reveal the speaker's intent, emotion, and even generational, educational, and cultural backgrounds.

However, words—and their use and misuse—are not limited to the speaker alone. They are shared by the listeners, both intended and unintended. I am fully aware that certain words can offend a listener due to their crudeness or vulgarity, and when my children were young, I censored my language.

I also often corrected them on the proper placement of pronouns in sentences. To their annoyance, I would feign confusion and make them rephrase sentences that were otherwise comprehensible, such as fixing "Me and my friends want to..." to "My friends and I want to..." This was not because I am rigidly bound by grammar and spelling rules. (My editors can attest to this, as they often mark up my submissions with gallons of red ink, highlighting my failures in adhering to proper language rules.) I did not raise my children to obsess over using "proper grammar" throughout their lives, and I don't care if they follow the rules as adults. My only intention was to make them aware that rules for formal English exist and to provide them with a foundation for understanding those standards. By respecting them, I now give them the freedom to playfully manipulate language in any creative way they desire, and I will listen with great interest and a smile.

Sailors use foul language without reservation, often seizing any opportunity for vulgarity and profanity and applying it liberally and enthusiastically. It may not be mature, clever, or insightful, but it is undeniably efficient and evocative. I loved it. It felt like the worst of the English language was being set free to bask in the light for a few moments. We were surrounded by sailors who behaved and spoke like sailors.

And what were we to do if we were offended?

Chastising, complaining, or admonishing would only frustrate our sailor, making her act in line with our wishes rather than her own. We were intruders in their world—were we supposed to change centuries of countercultural behavior by suddenly imposing our own moral standards? Not only would that be unjust, but it would also be ridiculous. If we couldn't handle a barrage of f-bombs, 'shits', and 'damns', then we had no business trespassing on their time together.

Nor should we expect our sailor to refrain from adopting this language. Just because she was raised to speak in a certain way doesn't mean she can't learn to talk differently. It may not be who she was before boot camp, and it may not be her behavior as she grows older, but in this moment of her career, around her peers, she uses foul language. She has essentially embraced the mannerisms of her new community.

To be fair, every sailor, including ours, apologized after their initial violation of what some might consider 'appropriate' language. Our sailor's first slip went unnoticed by her, and we chose to ignore it. The second slip was halted midway, her face turning red as she froze, the word "fu–" trailing off, the final consonants awkwardly lingering unsaid. I stared back at her, deliberately raising my eyebrows in anticipation, daring her to proceed while struggling not to laugh.

In that initial instance, and later when other sailors offered their own apologies after their first exclamation of foul language after meeting us, we quickly absolved them and dismissed any concerns. It was something that all three of us—including Little Sister, who is more sensitive to such language—had to accept. However, I was pleased to see that our sailor, along with many others, were still respectful of those around them; they acknowledged their social missteps and respected that those words can make some people uncomfortable.

It was important for us to spend the day with our sailor and her peers without any conflict or awkwardness. I wanted to be with them in a way that allowed them to feel comfortable being themselves. It didn't take long before we no longer noticed the colorful language or inappropriate jokes. Even the shock of seeing my daughter adopt this behavior passed easily. And while I was initially worried that Mom and Little Sister might have some issues overlooking this, it quickly became apparent that I had nothing to worry about. We all seemed to accept this as the new normal, and we had a great time.

Our reward for waking up early, navigating our way through the airport to connect with the sailors, and enduring the exhaustion of exploring the publicly-accessible areas of the airport was another day spent with our sailor among her friends. These were the amazing men and women who had freshly volunteered to serve our country. We got a glimpse behind the scenes and experienced a piece of their world.

Groups of sailors gathered and roamed the airport, visiting each other and coordinating goodbyes. They raced through the halls to find gates where other sailors were preparing to board their flights, to get in one final farewell. They huddled together in waiting areas and played card games. They shared meals. They aimlessly wandered in packs that grew and shrank, split and merged, as they looked for ways to pass the time until they departed.

We followed along, sometimes separate or off to the side and sometimes surrounded by men and women in dress blues. We learned about their histories and discussed their hopes for the future. We also met other families who, like us, had chosen to spend the day with their sailors. Throughout the experience, we felt as welcome as anyone else wearing Navy uniforms.

I relished every opportunity to meet a new sailor. Where

were they from? What was their rate? Why did they choose this life? They responded to my questioning with surprising enthusiasm, offering long monologues that provided insight into their lives, backgrounds, and aspirations.

I discovered that they were just like other young people we knew—kids from high school, church, our neighborhood, friends, nieces, and nephews. Some were searching for guidance and structure as they faced an uncertain future, while others were taking the first steps of a well-planned journey. For many, the Navy was the beginning of a new chapter in their lives, and for others, boot camp and "A" School were the initial stages of a long and successful military career.

They came from all over the country and multiple U.S. territories. They were raised in blue-collar families as well as families with financial means that offered different opportunities. Some had just finished high school, others had completed college, and some were leaving behind lives where they had already taken steps in starting other careers.

Each man and woman I met talked about home and their old lives, their families, friends, and loved ones, without any sense of sorrow. They didn't show any signs of homesickness or fear. Instead, they were resolute and confident, eagerly embracing this new adventure without hesitation.

They had chosen this new life—it had not been forced upon them. None of them were running away from their past or trying to escape their old identities. They weren't fulfilling any expectations or obligations. I knew that among them, there must be sailors who fit that description, but throughout the day, in each new sailor I met, I found someone who had chosen to serve not out of necessity, but with a clear purpose, marching proudly toward their future in the Navy.

Our sailor led us from gate to gate through the different

terminals as she said goodbye to the friends she had grown close to during boot camp. There were occasionally tears, but they were rare and failed to dampen the excitement that filled the sailors. Each goodbye held an unspoken agreement not to forget each other.

In my private and cynical thoughts, I wanted to feel sorry for the inevitably broken promises. I knew that all the sentiment in the world couldn't stop the separation that time brings. Communication would slowly dwindle and eventually cease, faces and names would become difficult to recall as the years passed, and eventually, that person's identity would become hazy or disappear altogether.

But what I hadn't considered was that it didn't really matter. That individual person was part of a collective that shaped our sailor's life, contributing to who she had become and who she would continue to be. They had gone through boot camp together; whether their names were remembered, or their faces remained clearly etched in our sailor's memory, they would always be there. It was the combined effort of all the recruits that supported and raised our sailor, becoming a part of her identity and her success. Having completed and conquered boot camp, she could move forward in her career as a stronger and more capable person, and each sailor she said goodbye to had helped her achieve this. Every step she took, every accomplishment she achieved, and every opportunity that came her way was possible because these people were a part of her initial success.

These friends had been there when our sailor hated things the most and when she was the proudest of herself she had ever been. Now they were moving forward, achieving their ambitions, heading to the next part of their training and to duty stations that would make them part of the United States Navy. Every single one of them owed a debt to the others and to the collective unit. Each departing sailor's achievement was due in part to the group's combined dedication to their success; each graduate was the product of the love and support of others. Whether they knew it or could articulate it, some part of them must have been able to see it in each other. I don't know what they were feeling, but it seemed to me that each goodbye was also a thank you, an appreciation for each other and what they had been through together. For myself, I was glad for them. And if I could, I would go back and thank each of them for being there, and for all they did for my sailor and the person she was becoming.

As the day progressed, the rushing from one part of the airport to the other slowed down. The times between farewells stretched longer. The group of sailors that joined us throughout the day became smaller, and time closed in on our goodbye.

We decided to have one final moment together—a nice dinner where we could sit at a proper table. After enduring long lines for fast food or portable meals, we were relieved to find an actual restaurant, called Stefani's Tuscany Café. We longed for a quieter and more enjoyable dining experience, and a sit-down dinner was exactly what we needed. Our group of sailors joined us, and together we filled a large table, ready to enjoy a delicious meal in the company of friends.

During dinner, the sailors' excitement was evident on their faces, undeterred by the long day of waiting, idling, and saying goodbye to friends. They joked and shared stories about RTC. More than anything, they spoke about their futures; they were filled with excitement and hope, looking forward to what lay ahead. They weren't dwelling on the lives they left behind. They hadn't given up or lost anything. They were gaining their futures, moving forward in their adventures, focused on the possibilities ahead of them.

This enthusiasm may fade over time. No one truly knows what challenges and obstacles will stand before them as they strive to achieve their hopes and dreams. I understand how life tends to get in the way. The older we get, the more we look back with pretend wisdom and the lies of experience. We know all this excitement and hope must be balanced with the expectation that something will get in their way, and not every challenge can be overcome. Some things will be difficult, even impossible—and for a moment, it was hard to hold this information back, to refrain from pointing out that not every sailor at that table would join the fleet. Success was not guaranteed; some would face defeat, pain, loss, and failure.

I knew this was likely, but I couldn't see it in their faces. Not then, not with those confident smiles and those excited eyes. The truth was they had experienced and accomplished things that I never could. Who was I to predict their futures? How could I assume their strength, training, and sense of purpose, which had already brought them so far, would not be enough to conquer any challenge?

These young men and women, who may have seemed like kids just months before, had already achieved so much. They had overcome trials and tests that I would never face. Their life experience and newfound discipline far surpassed what I had at twenty years old. They already possessed a work ethic and drive that took me years to develop. They had a strength and brotherhood that I had never been a part of. Life may chip away at who they are, but age, reason, and wisdom will build them up and make them strong.

Then a greater realization struck me: the people sitting with me, my wife, and two of my children were United States Navy Sailors. They had become warriors and protectors. Their mere presence in any ocean or location on Earth would hold a collective influence that impacts the geopolitical landscape. Their existence would inform the decisions made by leaders of other countries, as well as the generals and admirals commanding both friendly and hostile forces.

Each person at that table wearing their Navy uniforms would go on to join the fleet and assume their role in those calculations.

To be a part of the conversations, plans, strategies, and decisions made by the world's history-makers, they had to make the choice to serve and commit to that choice. These sailors had endured the Confidence Chamber, learned to fight fires in enclosed metal halls and tubs, and acquired lifesaving skills, weapons training, and many other necessary skills—and that was just the beginning of their journey toward becoming part of something greater. This was not the culmination of their journey; it was only the beginning. Yes, they were sailors now, but they were boarding those planes to become more than just sailors.

When I looked around the table, I realized who I was sharing dinner with, and I felt unworthy of the honor.

The final blow hit me later: my kid—the child we raised—was one of them. Not so long ago, I cradled her tiny infant body in my arms. I groaned when she peed on me as I changed her diaper. I looked into her innocent eyes as I fed her. As she grew, I watched her stumble, and fall. I saw small triumphs as milestones were reached.

And the years continued to pass.

I remembered Christmas morning when she woke up, looked at the tree filled with presents, and came to the devastating realization that Santa had come during the night but had moved on and wouldn't be there to meet her in the morning. I remember going on a school trip with her to South Carolina, where we spent the night on the USS *Yorktown*, which may have influenced her decision to join the Navy. We attended father-daughter dances, where we had the best time being the worst dancers. I cheered and shouted her name as she took the stage to accept her diploma.

I witnessed her proudest moments, celebrated even the

smallest achievements. We experienced first days and last days together. She was by my side when I held my father's hand as he passed away. I saw her at her best and loved her when she felt her worst. Through it all, I was her dad. I still am.

However, with the realization at that table, I no longer possessed the authority that comes with age and experience. She sat with the other sailors, whom I greatly admired and silently honored, as an esteemed peer. She was one of them, connected by the same skills and talents they had all acquired, refined, and mastered together.

Perhaps I didn't deserve a seat at their table. I hadn't earned my place. But it was my absolute pleasure and privilege to share a meal with them. Our daughter, on the other hand, deserved to be there. She had earned her spot at that table alongside her friends as a sailor.

And when it was time for us to say goodbye, it wasn't at the gate as she prepared to board the plane, but after the meal. We left them to spend those last few hours together on their own, knowing that we would see her again sooner than she would see many of them. We let remaining hours before the planes departed be reserved for the sailors.

10. After

What happens after the goodbye—whether it's the last hug at the PIR ceremony, after liberty, or at the airport—is unique to each sailor. The future months and years, their career, and when we will see our sailors again on leave, are not solely determined by their rate, "A" School, training, or how they join the fleet. It also depends on the choices they make as adults and how they navigate their path.

On the morning we said goodbye on the cracked black-top of that recruiting office parking lot, before boot camp or PIR, a great dark shadow hung over us. I feared that this departure would lead to other choices that would take my child further and further away from us. Her path could lead to a bright and exciting future, or be burdened by the consequences of poor decisions. This was the fear of the unknown.

When each of my children joined the military, it was tempting to focus on the positive possibilities, their immediate success, and the promise offered for their future. This could help ease the emptiness we felt when we realized they wouldn't be as close or a daily part of our lives. However, I also felt that maybe they weren't ready for this independence; they were young, and they lacked the experience and wisdom needed to make the right choices that would shape their future. After all, there was still so much they could learn from us. How could I guide them when they were so far away?

It was wonderful to witness their accomplishments and celebrate their successes. I was proud to see them become independent and capable members of our military. I consider it a great honor to proudly proclaim to anyone who will listen that my son is an airman and my daughter is a sailor. Both of my adult children serve in the United States Armed Forces, and I am proud of this fact.

At the same time, I quietly contend with significant fears. I worry about their mental health, physical well-being, and emotional state. Are they feeling alone, sad, or depressed? I wonder if they might need me but are too embarrassed, shy, or afraid to reach out and call. Do they feel pressured to live up to unrealistic expectations, or strive too hard for goals that may be beyond their abilities? Will the challenges they face lead to poor decisions, unhealthy coping mechanisms, or even self-harm?

Then there are the life problems that may arise. They could be harmed through no fault of their own. What if they fall in love with the wrong person, get married, have a child, and things don't work out, resulting in a divorce and the responsibility of caring for another human being? What if they decide to experiment with drinking or drugs and end up in an accident?

And there are the small choices, both good and bad, that can jeopardize their careers. Life is filled with pitfalls, both hidden and obvious, that can suddenly and irreversibly turn into tragedy. If those things were to happen, all the challenges they overcame to reach this point in their lives would have been endured for nothing.

In moments when they need us the most, they could be far away in another state, a different country, or floating in the middle of the ocean in a different hemisphere. If we were to become aware of a problem, we would be powerless to do anything. Suddenly, we would find ourselves waiting helplessly as our children face the world without our presence. Or we may hear about it after the fact, when their bad choices and someone else's terrible advice have already changed everything and there's nothing we can do.

These are the same fears any parent might have when

their child grows up and leaves home. Whether their kids go off to college, start a new career, or seek a fresh start, all parents will face these uncertainties. But my kids joined the military, adding an entire new set of concerns to the list. My children are part of an institution whose purpose is to prevent, engage in, and win wars.

I lose sleep worrying about things beyond our control. We live in a world with despots who possess indiscriminate weapons. There are countless madmen with violent followers who may target a military base, ship, or other facility where my sailor or airman may be stationed or passing through. I am terrified that someday my children may become my sacrifice.

As I write this, our nation is not directly involved in any war. However, I vividly remember the horror of September 11, 2001, when faceless monsters I had never heard of before attacked us on a clear blue morning in New York. Those of us who lived through that monumental moment in history understand how vulnerable we can be when we feel safe. Even as I watched from Florida, I could feel the towers fall. The entire planet shook under the violence of that attack. It showed me that the transition from complacency to war can happen in an instant, and it may be my children facing that conflict when it occurs again.

And if the day comes, I don't want to be a heroic parent who gave one of my greatest gifts to our nation. I don't want to bury my son or daughter in a flag-draped coffin. I don't want a twenty-one-gun salute, full military honors, and a thinly proclaimed sentiment alluding to some great debt our nation cannot pay. That's not what I signed up for when my children enlisted.

Was it?

I know there is a statistical probability that the chances of such things happening to my children are small. I once used this logic when explaining to my mother how no

aircraft carrier or submarine has been seriously damaged
from an attack since World War II. The last time a U.S.
Navy ship was attacked was the USS *Cole*, a guided missile
destroyer, in October 2000. This occurred before most new
enlistees, including my daughter, were even born. The hor-
rific result of the *Cole* bombing is part of the simulation our
sailors endure during the Battle Stations test they need to
pass in order to graduate boot camp.

But even as my arguments are passed off as factoids to
reassure my mother that her grandkids will be safe, it
doesn't help me. No statistics will help. If anything, I wonder if we are overdue for another tragedy, and that sends
my fear skyrocketing.

I know these feelings are irrational, but they are still jus-
tifiable concerns. The low likelihood of these things happening does not diminish the anxiety. The possibility of
something horrible happening to our loved ones is what
leads to caution and planning. We treat the absurdly rare
events as realistic and likely so that if they ever do happen,
we are prepared.

But parents usually have some measure of control they
can make ready for. We teach kids to take care when in
kitchens and to avoid hot stoves. We tell them not to talk
to strangers, check in with us, don't ignore our calls, check
their rearview mirrors, and buckle up. And when they fail
or do stupid things, we admonish those mistakes so that
larger ones don't happen.

But how do we prepare for those threats outside the
control or influence of us or our sailors? So much agency is
stripped from us by the choice to join the military that we
feel as though the future is now out of our hands. How can
we feel like we have any ability to help when they are beyond our reach or guidance?

Accepting the things beyond our control does not alle-
viate our fears or concerns. It does not make watching the

news any less stressful. It will never assuage the ever-present parental worries that permeate my solitary thoughts. I am utterly surrounded by news and promises of impending threats to my children that I cannot protect them from.

When one country invades another, or when one world leader starts puffing out their chest and presenting some frightening new posture, we look on, hoping things don't escalate. Car accidents, strange and unknown medical conditions, or an unbelievably bad and horrible day are all things that kill or maim people every day, and no one is ever "safe." But our kids being placed in harm's way because a war must be fought feels like they are courting danger.

We have no more control, and our influence over our sailors is reduced. I accept this unhappily, but completely. In this situation, I have only one thing I can control: I am the architect of my own response, and how my response to this new normal will affect my relationship with my children and, hopefully, allow some bit of influence to guide them when they need it the most. It may be subtle enough a weight to tip the scales for our sailor when she makes decisions. And when that influence cannot or does not affect their choices, we can be there to help with the consequences.

This becomes our biggest and most significant role as parents. We need to be available and accessible to these new adults as they assume their own independence. We can help guide our family through turbulent times and lift them up when they have fallen low. We can help them assume control of their own lives when external things wrest control from them. We can be there for them; despite the miles separating us. My role as a parent isn't affected by this distance, and my relationship with my kids is no less strong. The biggest change is how I approach my role: trusting that my kids will carry on the lessons and influence my wife and I provided through the years, while we remain ready, willing, and able to listen and provide encouragement when they need it.

I reflect on the time I left home to live on my own. I recall the sense of freedom and the immense responsibility that came with it. I remember both my triumphs and my mistakes. What stands out the most, however, is the realization that I needed my parents more than ever when I was separated from them. Although I often disregarded their advice, believing myself to be a self-sufficient adult who had all the answers, what truly mattered was knowing they were there for me. They would always be there—no matter how dire the situation. My parents were always the ones I could turn to.

Furthermore, my parents gave me the tools I needed to be an independent adult. They helped me define my moral compass, and they taught me to plan for and accept the consequences of my actions. I learned personal and social responsibility from them. I was prepared for my journey because of them. And I knew that while I may chart my own course, I would always have their help.

I want my children to experience that same sense of security, to have confidence even when I'm fearful of how little control I have over their well-being. I am there for them, even when the world seems to be against them.

Just as when I left home, the physical distance doesn't matter. My parents were miles away in another city, and my father didn't even have a functioning car. Moreover, I wasn't always the best son to my mother. Yet none of that mattered. I knew they were always just a phone call away. Nothing in the world would have stopped them. And nothing will stop me either.

11. A World Apart

It wasn't long after returning home that we settled into our new normal. Once again, we felt the vacancy, the emptiness that existed with one less person in a house accustomed to four. While that emptiness took some time to get used to, we were able to adjust to our day-to-day rhythm rather quickly. We moved forward. Work went well. My wife went back to school at night, while progressing forward in her own career. Little Sister adapted to life at home as the only child. I started thinking about this book.

We spent a couple of weeks packing up the remainder of our sailor's room, sorting some things into longer-term storage and setting aside other things we knew she might want at school. She was committed to this course now, so it made sense that we should embrace this change. We renovated the space, creating a new guest room that would be nice for any visitor but that also celebrated our kid's service through small touches. We even mounted the anchor decoration we used at the Navy Lodge, as well as an Air Force plaque. This had the two-fold effect of creating a space our kids can come home to while removing the constant reminder of their absence.

The vacuum of space left by people who no longer lived there was being filled with a promise of opportunity. A room not committed to any single person's identity made for a place that invited our children to come home. It was a room that looked forward to their visits, rather than missed their presence.

Furthermore, working on the room gave us something we could all participate in. Being a part of transitioning that space was a nice way to externalize the changes happening to our family. We defined our participation, but we also provided insights and suggestions so that we could each see our contribution to the new room. It was our space now, waiting openly for them to come and fill it, even if only for a few days.

During her training, our sailor would still be coming home for some visits. We expected the most likely times would be after graduation from each of her training segments. "A" School for her rate would be six months—but she was a Navy Nuke, which meant "A" School would be followed by six more months of Naval Nuclear Power School (NNPS), then another six months of prototype training at one of two Nuclear Power Training Units (NPTUs). Add in some breaks and delays between classes, and she would be in South Carolina for over eighteen months. She would be housed on base for the first two schools, but when she got to prototype training, she would need her own apartment.

Once she arrived at "A" School, we were able to have more or less regular communication. Phone calls, text messages, and even the occasional video call allowed us the chance to properly connect with our sailor. Life at her new base was both complex and familiar. She was learning to navigate her responsibilities and was building new relationships and friendships. She was happily settling into her new life.

It was surprising to me how normal things can suddenly become. Sporadic phone calls and text messages didn't replace dinner conversations and daily updates, but they were a close second that seamlessly took on their own normalcy, as though this was how things were always supposed to be. Maybe they were. This is the natural evolution of our relationships with our children. But seeing how the emptiness suddenly fills itself was a bittersweet relief.

But life doesn't like to stay normal or quiet for long.

Eventually, like all adults, there are problems, and parents get phone calls that are hard to listen to. These are made even more difficult when the situations are immediate and it feels like they need us there with them, beside them, ready to help and support them in their hour of need. Frustratingly, I found myself unable to do that. I couldn't be there in time.

Our sailor was at least a six-hour drive away (and not much better by plane). Travel to our airman would require a twelve-hour flight halfway across the world. I felt useless, unable to help. Worse, I had believed that when my kids needed me, nothing would stop me from getting to them—but when I was tested, I didn't so much fail as come face-to-face with a reality that wouldn't let me live up to my own expectations. And how could I? If they needed me to be with them, I wouldn't be able to reach them any sooner than half a day, and my son would need to wait an entire day under the best circumstance; by then, any help I could provide would be superficial at best. I had promised myself that when called, I'd stand beside my kids. Now I realized how impossible that would be. The truth was, they would stand alone.

We faced how useless the distances and time made us feel. But I also underestimated my children's capabilities. They didn't need me right there when all hell was breaking loose, and it wasn't a realistic expectation regardless of whether they lived down the street or a twelve-hour flight across the Pacific Ocean. We spent their lives preparing them to be self-sufficient, to problem-solve, to accept responsibility for their choices, and to be prepared for the consequences of their actions. My kids were capable. Their parents did their job. I like to think we did that job well.

But that didn't stop them from reaching out to us when they did run into problems, and it didn't mean they weren't asking for help. And when they did come to us with their troubles, I fully realized how much our roles as parents had changed: we became allies, resources for support, potential affirmation, and validation. We could provide additional insights, alternative points of view, even some gentle criticism if it was wanted, asked for, or warranted.

Our sailor and airman were young adults, prone to mistakes due to ignorance and inexperience but capable of handling the consequences of their actions. When faced with unforeseen problems, they could identify and choose their own path to resolve them. However, we began to worry about the distance, time, and feelings of loneliness and isolation .

During one of our phone calls with our sailor, we learned the sad news that someone at their school had attempted to end their own life. That was unexpected, but what surprised us even more was that this wasn't the first attempt, although it was one of the rare ones that failed. This was difficult to hear.

What drives people to those extremes? What pressures, expectations, or fears lead them to consider such drastic measures? I couldn't comprehend being driven to that definitive act, but my concern was whether it could happen to my children. If they struggled with the demands of their training or job, many other options should be available. But if their hopes and dreams are tied to their military careers, or if they feel pressure due to familial obligations, and they see no way forward, would a fatal solution be something they may consider?

Concerns about mental health in the military were well-known to us. Numerous reports and studies had shown disturbing trends that our family had discussed many times, and some schools and jobs within the Navy were known to have a significant impact on sailors' mental health. While we had talked to our kids about mental health awareness, we hadn't considered what seeking help in the military would actually entail, or what it might cost them. The Department of Defense was working to address these concerns, but there were real and current problems that needed to be considered.

Our sailor explained that some sailors were being separated from the Navy due to mental health issues. Those who sought help, were stressed, or had underlying problems could be prescribed treatment—usually medication—that would ultimately disqualify them from service. While we always encouraged our kids to get the help they needed in the military, we now saw a problem where concerns for mental health directly conflicted with the sailors' jobs.

The concerns were haunting, especially when so much was affecting the mental health of both of my kids serving. We could see the changes happening to them—the concern, the stress, the pressure, and the effects these had on them. And we started to worry.

But it wasn't realistic to assume that the responsibility to preserve their mental health was entirely dependent on them. Nor was it reasonable to expect the military to be accountable for every aspect of a serving individual's mental health. In fact, I believe that putting such an expectation on individuals and institutions may be more dangerous than helpful. Isn't it more practical to assume that they are only part of a larger solution, which should also include the support of family, friends, and other loved ones?

We discussed the problem as a family, recognizing that this was an issue that required all of us to be involved at equal levels. Our kids were not just our children with respect to this issue; instead, we were five adults. Even though Little Sister was 16 at the time, the legal age of majority didn't apply. This was an issue where mental and emotional responsibility were the defining elements of our perspective, and so in this respect, all of us were capable of contributing to the dialog.

The five of us came together to support each other as a family, focused on sustaining each other. It required a mutual level of understanding and respect, as well as a recognition that we needed to preserve confidence and trust. It meant being available, without judgment. It meant keeping each other's secrets, even from the rest of the group. It was imperative that they seek help—whether from a parent or a sibling—and know that their conversations would be confidential, even from their mom, dad, or both.

As parents, we would keep this trust, even from each other. I didn't think this was fair to the parents; keeping secrets from each other is not something my wife and I feel very comfortable doing. But I believed this was fair to our kids. Our kids required this level of trust and confidence in their parents; they needed to know that their privacy was valued and respected. What mattered to me was that when my kids weren't comfortable coming to me, I hoped they would feel able to reach out to my wife, whom I absolutely, unconditionally, and unwaveringly trusted. If not us, then the next best and most trusted resource was each other. Having these pathways for confidential conversations gave our kids multiple ways to get help from us if they needed it.

We also started having scheduled weekly calls. Every Sunday night, we would meet over a video call and visit with each other. There was no agenda; it was simply a chance for the five of us to see each other, talk, joke, catch up, and enjoy the company of our family. If someone had a rough day or week, we could talk about it. We could also celebrate each other's victories.

The calls were usually short—around thirty minutes, and rarely as much as an hour. By meeting weekly, we only had a small amount of catching up to do. If someone had a difficult week and needed to unload, there was plenty of room for them to speak openly and for as long as they needed. Five people came together each week, each having four allies who were ready to love us, support us, and listen to us.

Most importantly, to listen.

While this wouldn't eliminate all problems, it did open up opportunities for all of us to help. Our kids reached out on various issues. When they did, it was usually because they needed a sympathetic ear. They wanted someone who loves them to hear and listen to them. Those calls and conversations were a reminder that we were there for them, that they were supported; they might be far away, but they were never alone, and they could always come home.

While the weekly calls, affirmations, and frequent conversations helped, we also reminded them that if things ever got really bad or dark, or they started feeling like things were getting beyond what they could handle, they would need to seek out professional resources. Mental health professionals are healthcare providers. I wouldn't want anyone except a dentist to go near my teeth with a drill, nor would I ever allow anyone but a doctor to operate on me, set a broken bone, or give me a medical diagnosis. Parents and loved ones who don't have the training, resources, or professional experience aren't equipped or qualified to provide adequate care in mental health, nor should we feel like we are capable of taking on that responsibility—the consequences of being wrong could be just as fatal as in any other medical field, and the seriousness of that should be respected.

That being said, there are multiple paths to get help. Therapist and psychologist, both private and through the armed services, are available. But if there are concerns that these services may affect their career, service men and women can also get help through chaplains. Chaplains are often considered the first line of defense for service member's mental health. Regardless of the nature of a person's faith or belief in God, a chaplain's responsibility is to the sailor's well-being, and they can be essential tools in helping overcome mental and emotional struggle.

If getting the help our kids need would require medicine or other treatment that would disqualify them from military service, then so be it. There are other options for their future. There will be other jobs, professions, and accomplishments they could be a part of. I would rather have them safe, alive, and separated from the Air Force or Navy than mourn the loss of our airman or sailor. They are worth so much more to me than their jobs.

While it was important for them to hear all this from us, it was also vital that our weekly conversations weren't constant reminders of our own insecurities as parents. Weekly calls were about visiting with them, showing our love and support, not browbeating them with public service announcements. Instead, these calls became regular virtual gatherings. Through these visits, we saw that our children were owning their own worlds, their lives, and their experiences. We were tuning in for the latest episode of our family.

They faced challenges, but they overcame them. Sometimes, those difficulties weighed heavily on them. There were times when the question "How was your week?" was answered by a sad "It's been a rough week, to be honest." But when they needed real help, they reached out to each other, and sometimes their mother, and sometimes their dad. And we were there for them. We also listened for those subtle and sometimes unspoken moments when they needed affirmation, love, and support.

But the calls were more often opportunities to see them smile. And they smiled so much. They might have missed us, but they never seemed homesick. They had found their own place, made a new home for themselves. I was meeting with my adult kids every week.

And after each call ended, I was reminded how our relationship with them is constantly changing. While this evolution can be intimidating, I also found it very comforting. They had grown up, moved on to adulthood, and embraced their lives enthusiastically. They found new hobbies and adventures outside of the military. They were scubadiving old shipwrecks, spending weekends at beach retreats, skydiving from airplanes, and so much more. They filled their weekends and holidays with new and exciting experiences. They are fully and completely living their lives in the best years to live them.

My kids didn't know it, but their adventures sometimes remind me that I have also matured. I have grown older as I inch closer to growing old. And as the years behind me start to outnumber the years ahead of me, I can't help but look back and see my own life and the stories that filled it.

There was a version of me before my kids, years peppered with the escapades of the irresponsible and stupid. Somehow, they don't seem to matter; those years were my adolescence. Then I became a father and a husband. In the years that followed, they filled vacancies in my life I could not have known existed. Before I knew it, the only stories worth telling became the ones they made with me. There was a point where the adult version of me started, and that line was drawn by them.

Someday, my airman and sailor will look back on their own lives and tell their own stories. Those early adventures won't start with leaving home. They won't talk about basic training or boot camp. They won't waste words on everything that happened to them during training, while we waited at home for each short phone call or the rare letter delivered in the mail. Those days would contain the least interesting things they did in their adult lives. How their family survived their training won't even be mentioned in the tales of their lives. The story of their adult years started after graduation; boot camp and basic training were just an epilogue to their childhood.

And even after graduating to adulthood and claiming their independence, they still found a place for their parents and their family. We may be miles, oceans, or a world apart, but we are still together, connected by our shared history, our love, and the strength and support we give each other. I feel just as connected to my kids now as I have throughout their childhood. While so much has changed, it is also very much the same. How we connect, and how often, may be different, but the connection remains unbroken and stronger than ever.

More importantly, I have come to terms with their independence. Over time, I have become increasingly aware of how 'adult' my adult children really are. While nothing will ever replace having them at home, watching them take on the world on their own is very exciting. I am humbled by their strength, their commitment to their future and our country, and their service.

As I reach the end of this story, I find that I have expressed—maybe even gushed about—how proud I am to be the parent of an airman and a sailor. That is definitely true in an uncomplicated way. The deeper truth—what I think I really mean in those expressions of love—is that I am proud to be the parent of strong, capable, and independent adults, two of whom happen to be an airman and a sailor. I'm just the lucky person who gets to be their dad.

Part 2 – The Family Boot Camp Guide

"There's this misconception that the Navy is this cruise ship, and you get to go out and sail around, and every now and then, you have to swab the deck. But, no, it is a very impressive group of young people that live at sea, in this place that's very uncomfortable. They exude a pride that is well-deserved."

– Tom Hanks

01. Embrace the Suck

One of the most popular military phrases is also one of the best pieces of advice for dealing with a less-than-ideal situation. "Embrace the suck" reminds us that things will be difficult, and that situations don't really care for our comfort or happiness. Our best chance for success is to accept the reality we are experiencing, and overcome it with good planning, fortitude, and a positive attitude.

This phrase perfectly captures the frustration and confusion our family experienced trying to navigate our daughter's initial steps into her Navy career, and how we confronted those difficulties. While we have many happy memories from this period, there was also a lot of frustration and fear. Information was both scarce and way too abundant. We could go online and ask a question and get ten answers. But what was correct? What was outdated? And what about the questions we didn't ask? While online resources can be phenomenal (and I reference some of my favorites in this book), they also expose the weaknesses of farming social media and websites for help. You can get the answer to your question, but you won't get the whole story.

Part 2 of this book is intended to help you with these challenges. It is the product of my family's successful efforts in planning and navigating the time before our daughter left for boot camp, her journey at RTC, and our eventual trip to celebrate her success at PIR. But it is also the accumulated knowledge we gained in hindsight and the information we wish we had acquired earlier in order to prevent or avoid some of our difficulties.

To make things easier, I have tried to maintain consistency in the ordering of this section in relation to the chapters in Part 1: Our Story. The focus of this guide is on the needs of the family and to provide some help in preparation for this journey. Families should navigate these suggestions together, offering their own input on things such as packing lists, notable sights in Chicago, and what responsibilities they are willing to assume.

In our family, it was beneficial to involve everyone in the

planning process, but only to the extent that they desired. Some members may be indifferent about activities in Chicago, leaving you or someone else to make all decisions on what to see or where to eat. However, by presenting options from a list, individuals may express preferences for things they are more interested in. It is not recommended to push anyone to participate. Enthusiasm cannot be forced. The lack of interest from a partner, child, or friend may stem from genuine indifference, or it may reflect underlying emotions related to a loved one leaving home. If someone declines involvement, respect their decision and move forward without their help on that subject.

Also, I don't recommend making all your plans at once. Focus on smaller tasks or singular goals, such as arranging transportation to Chicago, in one conversation with your family. Addressing other details and discussions in subsequent days can prevent feeling overwhelmed and making hasty decisions. It may be helpful to view tasks as a checklist of goals, utilizing each section of this guide accordingly. One such list is available for download, printing, or electronic use at www.underwaybook.com/resources.

Take your time planning. Typically, you will have several weeks or months before your loved one departs for boot camp, and another 10 weeks or so until their boot camp graduation. Use this time to address packing lists and other items in the section labeled "Before Boot Camp." If you have additional time before departure, continue progressing through your plans. Otherwise, focus on travel arrangements, accommodations, and other logistics while your loved one is in training.

If you read Part 1 of this book, you may notice discrepancies between the information presented here and our family's experience. This is due to the limited information we had during our journey. It was only after experiencing the process that we realized certain aspects were missing from our planning or should have been done in a different order. For instance, we packed our sailor's belongings when she had liberty from "A" School during the holidays, when it would have been more appropriate to do so before she left for boot camp. These adjustments have been reflected in the corresponding lists presented here.

You should also keep in mind that it is impossible for one book to fully anticipate every question or incorporate the latest information. Online communities and websites are usually kept up to date by a wide range of volunteers including active duty or retired military and their family members. I have listed our favorite social media groups, websites, and video pages that were invaluable to our journey at www.underwaybook.com/resources. If you are in a position to assist some of the privately managed pages, please consider a small donation to support their efforts. There should be links on their websites.

Finally, remember that you aren't alone. At times, you may feel frustrated and afraid. Answers and information may seem nebulous and overwhelming. Lean on the wonderful communities of the Navy family. More importantly, rely on your own family. It's okay to tell your partner, your children, or anyone who will listen that you miss your sailor. It's okay to say that this period is hard for you. It's even okay to hate it. But the best way to support your sailor, and take enjoyment where you can, is to prepare and plan. And for those things beyond your control is where you embrace the suck.

02. Preparing for Departure

Your recruiter will handle most of the planning and preparation for the sailor regarding boot camp. This section deals with elements that should be addressed prior to the recruit's departure by the family.

Primary Point of Contact

Your recruit will need to choose a Primary Point of Contact (PPOC). The PPOC is the first one listed as the recruit's emergency contact. It is also the person who will be reached out to first for important information by the recruit. When phone calls are available to them, they will call the PPOC's number. The PPOC should never have their phone set to Do Not Disturb (DND). If they must turn off their phone, or turn on DND mode, forward calls to another person.

Determine a "Bad News Rule"

It's possible unforeseen and tragic events may occur while the recruit is at RTC. It is a good idea to lay out some rules regarding if, and when, a recruit is informed of bad news. Sometimes, this information can add additional pressure, stress, and distractions to their training. For instance, if a loved one is in an accident but is otherwise healthy, it might not be a good idea to convey this information. However, if an immediate family member is badly hurt, extremely ill, or even passes away, the recruit may want to be informed. Think of the information in tiers such as:

- Immediate Family (spouse/parent/sibling/family pet)

- Extended Family (grandparent, aunt/uncle, cousin)

- Boyfriend/Girlfriend

- Close Friend(s)

Meanwhile, the severity of the information may also be a factor. For instance, a life-changing injury, illness, or death may be something they will want to know regarding immediate family, but not with close friends. Defining the seriousness of the information should be considered for each relationship type.

Establish an Account Manager

The recruit should appoint someone to log in on their behalf to any online accounts that might need to be managed or monitored while they are at RTC. These would be any accounts that have regular billing, like paid subscriptions, bank accounts, insurance accounts, etc. The recruit will need to change the passwords (don't provide the current passwords) to something the account manager can use. The account manager will need to regularly check these accounts and verify the authenticity of any transactions. If there is suspicious behavior, the account manager should suspend or cancel the account. The sailor can reset passwords after PIR.

The account manager will also store any important letters or other mail for the recruit. This may include opening and replying to any official mail in case there are deadlines for response. For instance, the account manager should handle mail from colleges, banking institutions, and bills.

Handle Online Accounts

Get a list of accounts that can be suspended and suspend them. This includes subscription accounts that bill regularly. But also consider locking or suspending social media accounts, utilities that may not be needed, or accounts that can be canceled. Some common things are:

- Streaming services
- Magazine subscriptions

- Standing or pre-booked appointments such as salon, hair, or medical appointments
- Gym memberships

Setup Autopay

Set up autopay where applicable. The sailor should take any recurring bills that can't be suspended and have them set to autopay where possible. Common bills might include:

- Cell phone bills
- Vehicle insurance
- Credit card payments

Initial PIR Plans

Plan for liberty after PIR. Included in the preparations for PIR are clothing options for the sailor in case they want to relax in the hotel in their civilian clothes. Take this time to plan for that eventuality and set aside the clothes they choose for that occasion. Don't forget to include any important items they might want access to during their liberty. For instance, we packed our sailor's ukulele. She was able to enjoy it during liberty, but it did come back home with us.

PIR Guest List

Work with your recruit to make a list of up to 8 possible family, friends, and other loved ones who can attend their boot camp graduation ceremony. The list should be in order of importance, prioritizing the top 4 people your recruit wants to attend at the top. If, for any reason, anyone in the top 4 can't make it to the graduation ceremony, work your way down the list for anyone else who may want to attend. Keep in mind that anyone can go to Illinois to visit your sailor during their liberty (if your sailor has liberty to leave base). However, only 3-4 people will be able to attend the PIR ceremony.

Pack Their Room/Space

It will be a long time before they come home for any extended period longer than a week or two. It's a good idea for them to pack accordingly. Important items should be packed separately. These would be items they might want when they get to "A" School. Then pack items they will want when they get their place after "A" School or reach their first duty station. Finally, keep long-term storage separate. These will be items the sailor doesn't want to donate or throw away but will not take with them on their Navy adventure.

We recommend using colored masking tape to clearly mark the boxes. For instance, blue tape may be for "A" School or short-term storage, white tape for once they get settled, and all other items are for long-term storage. Set the short-term storage items aside for now in an easily accessible place.

Some parents may balk at this. They may argue that the recruit will be gone for months and packing their items away may not be necessary at this point. However, this packing requires the sailor's input. After they graduate and move on to "A" School, they may not be able to assist with packing items to be sent to them. Have the recruit identify those items now to make it easier for everyone before they leave for boot camp. Things will only get more complicated if you wait.

Sandboxx List

During boot camp, your recruit will be asked to provide a list of contacts including family and friends for communication with them while they are at RTC. You may consider defining this list ahead of time. Everyone on the list provided to the Navy will be sent information for downloading and using Sandboxx.

Sandboxx is an incredible service. However, it can be costly for some people who may not know they can send letters to your recruit via traditional mail. It's a good idea to only include people on the list who you have spoken with regarding using this service versus traditional mail. Usually, you will only include close family and friends who you expect will be communicating frequently with your recruit.

For everyone else, keep some extra mailing labels with you so you can hand them out to extended family or friends. This will make things more convenient for the sender, but also ensure that letters will be sent to the correct address.

03. Resources

Websites and online social media communities can be very helpful in navigating the Navy, RTC, and PIR. Connecting with other families currently going through the process can help you stay informed of changes and updates. Additionally, parents and family members in these groups can provide valuable clarification and support.

Underway Book Website Resource Page
www.underwaybook.com/resources

The website for this book has a section for resources, which includes links to the websites and pages below. Expect this page to be updated after this book's publication with any new information. While visiting, check the downloads section. It includes a checklist for getting your recruit and your family ready for boot camp, RTC, and the family trip to Great Lakes for PIR.

The Navy Dads and Navy for Moms Websites
www.navydads.com and www.navyformoms.ning.com

These sites offer fantastic resources for parents and loved ones, with detailed information, updated news, event information, and extremely helpful resources. Be sure to also join their Facebook groups.

Military Times YouTube Playlist "Becoming a Sailor"
www.youtube.com/@MilitaryTimesOnline/playlists

This playlist features short videos showing life at RDC. Navigate to Playlists and find "Becoming a Sailor" to get a peek into life at boot camp and see what your sailor will be experiencing.

Boot Camp Website
www.bootcamp.navy.mil

This is an official U.S. government website that contains the latest information, restrictions, rules, and other details for sailors and their families. You can find the current division graduation dates as well as up to date information on training schedules, additional family guides, and care packages that can be ordered for your recruit.

RTC Facebook Page
www.facebook.com/NavyRecruitTrainingCommand

This page provides news, information, and videos of graduation ceremonies. Our sailor was part of a performance division, so we were able to watch some of the graduation ceremonies she performed in. It also helped us get an idea of what to expect during PIR.

Sandboxx
www.sandboxx.us

The Sandboxx website and app allow you to connect with your sailor while they are at boot camp. You can send letters, pictures, newsletters, daily quotes, and stamps to your sailor through the app. While we personally chose a more traditional approach to sending letters, many parents find this method easier. We did find it helpful for checking the weekly updates on what they are doing in boot camp.

My Navy Taxi / Sarge's Meet and Greet
www.mynavytaxi.com

This is a popular transportation resource that also hosts a meet and greet for families of graduating sailors the night before PIR. Unfortunately, we discovered this too late and were unable to attend the dinner. We did meet a few parents who were able to attend the event who spoke quite highly of meet and greet.

Etsy PIR Anchors
www.etsy.com

Other sites like Amazon may have personalized anchors available, but Etsy has the widest variety. Search for "Navy PIR Anchors" and you're sure to find something amazing. If you are crafty, you can usually find blank wood anchors ready for the family to add their own signature style to.

All Hands Live Stream Page
www.allhands.navy.mil/Media/Live-Stream

The magazine of the U.S. Navy's media live-stream page includes streams of boot camp graduation videos as they occur. This is a great resource for family and friends who want to watch the event but aren't able to attend Great Lakes. Scroll down the page to find a listing of upcoming events. You can share the link for your sailor's specific PIR date with friends and family.

RTC Public Affairs YouTube Channel
www.youtube.com/@RTCPublicAffairs

Videos of past RTC graduation ceremonies are available here. You can also find other videos showcasing the training your sailors may be undergoing. After finding the video for your sailor's Pass in Review ceremony you can share it to your social media accounts and bookmark it for later reference. However, keep in mind that these videos may not be there forever. If you want to have a copy of the video, be sure your sailor orders a copy of the DVD when ordering their graduation photos.

Mental Health Resources
For general support and to find mental health resources in your area contact the Psychological Health Resource Center at www.health.mil/phrc
For crisis intervention call **988 then press 1** or visit: www.veteranscrisisline.net

Chaplain Services
www.netc.navy.mil/Commands/Naval-Service-Training-Command/NSTC-Headquarters/Chaplain
Chaplains can be contacted through the chain of command, the chaplain office, or through the sailor's workspace. Chaplains offer both spiritual and mental health support.

04. Correspondence

Communicating with your recruit is very important. Even if your recruit says they don't need letters before departing, assume they will change their mind. Boot camp is hard, and having a kind word, expressions of love, and support from home can make a huge difference in their mental health. When your recruit is having a rough time, you will want them to be able to reach into their stash of letters (or more importantly find the latest one they haven't read yet) and find the encouragement they need.

However, letter writing can be difficult to keep up with. Here are some tips to help you and your family keep the letters flowing.

Start Writing Your Letters Early

There's no reason why you have to wait until your recruit leaves for boot camp before writing your letters. In the time before their departure, you may want to capture your feelings, hopes, and words of encouragement and have these sentiments among the first correspondence sent to your recruit. You'd be surprised at how helpful writing letters can be to settle the anxiousness and excitement you may be feeling prior to their departure.

Don't Send Your Letters Too Soon

Although you can write early, you won't be able to send them until you receive a form letter from your recruit. These letters take about 2 weeks or so after they have arrived at boot camp. There may be delays, especially if your recruit isn't assigned to a division right away. Your recruit may send a letter early. It is tempting to respond to this letter by mailing it to the return address on that envelope. However, recruits will often spend some time at a different address than their final official address. You can go ahead and write a response, but don't send it just yet. If you send a letter without the correct information from the form letter, it may not go to the correct address or delivery will be delayed, or the letter may not reach your recruit at all.

Prepare Envelopes in Advance

Stock up on envelopes and stamps early. To save time and effort, print or order address labels with your address, and your recruit's address (this should be on the form letter sent after they are assigned to a division). Pre-stamp and label the envelopes ahead of time and set them in a place that's accessible to the family. When anyone writes a letter to be sent, they should drop it in the envelope (but don't seal it). Every morning you should check the current envelope. If there is something inside, seal it, date the back, and deposit the envelope in the outgoing mail.

Number or Date Envelopes

The Navy doesn't deliver letters as they arrive. Usually, they are delivered in clumps. This can lead to confusion if your recruit opens letters that reference events or news mentioned in a previous letter they have not opened yet. In order for your recruit to know in which order their letters should be read, write the date, or a sequence number on the back of the envelope.

No Cliffhangers

Don't include any news or updates about your family that might be incomplete until you know more. For example, a letter about a medical test, the family dog ran away, and you still haven't found it, some good news might be coming but we won't say more are all terrible things to do to your recruit. Again, letters may not arrive in a specific order. So, giving news about something that will need to be expanded on later can be cruel. You don't want your recruit waiting in anticipation for a resolution to some mystery you alluded to in your last letter. Just wait until things are resolved and give the full story.

Don't Pester Them to Write

Recruits are typically restricted by how much time or how often they will be able to write. Initially they will only have time on "holiday routine." This is usually on Sunday mornings and non-training days. Divisions may earn or lose time to write letters based on performance. Furthermore, these letter writing times are an opportunity for them to rest, and they very well might take it.

It can be tough not hearing from them but be patient and understanding. Remember, it is important that they hear words of support and encouragement from you. Don't expect a lot of communication back from them, and don't convey any pressure or sense of expectation from you. This is a difficult time for them, and they don't need their stress compounded with pressure from home.

Keep Them Short

If you are having trouble composing letters with any frequency you may consider not writing as much in each letter. A good long letter is nice from time to time, but it might be easier for your recruit to receive letters in smaller, more bite-sized chunks. A few paragraphs are all it takes.

Who says it has to be a letter?

If your recruit likes sports, print or clip a news article or sports scores for them and send those with a quick note. Read an interesting article or news story? What about that funny meme someone sent you? All of these can be printed and sent to them with a quick hand-written note to give the item context. For instance, if you watched an exciting game, find a news article about it. Print it out. At the top of the article, you might write "This was a great game! I really missed not watching it with you, but I thought you'd like this."

If you don't have a printer, you can send them via Sand-boxx. If you go this route, plan to buy packages of letters to save some money.

Set a Regular Letter Time

I have found it easier to write something quickly before bed at night. If I come across something in the news or a story I want to share with my recruit, I simply open my lap-top, print it out, and stuff it in an envelope. If something interesting happened that day, I wrote about it. It usually only took a few minutes, and then I was off to bed.

Alternate Writing Responsibilities

My wife wrote almost every day, even though she didn't have to. I'd usually write or send something every other day. It's nice for the recruit to receive something from the family daily or every few days. This can be easily achieved by alternating or assigning days for letter writing between people. By preparing envelopes in advance, you can quickly check each night before bed. If there is nothing there, put something, a letter, clipping, or picture in the envelope. If you did write something but found someone has already put something in the next outgoing envelope, put your letter in the envelope for the following day.

Young Writers Should Send Letters Less Frequently

Most young siblings may not be prolific writers and might struggle to maintain a regular letter-writing schedule. Having them send something once a week will be more than sufficient. Very young siblings can simply draw a picture or color something for their older brother or sister. It is helpful to plan special times for this, such as a Saturday morning letter writing time after breakfast. The family can gather at the dining room table, where the youngest can write, color, or draw pictures to send to their older sibling.

Send Mailing Labels

Some families may send self-addressed and stamped

envelopes. This can save some time, and may make things a little bit easier for your recruit. However, most of the envelopes won't be used. Instead, send your recruit labels with your address. This will save them time and prevent unused stamps and envelopes from going to waste.

Have your recruit provide a list of anyone not receiving letters.

There may be recruits who are not receiving letters. You can include an extra letter in your correspondence or send something directly to that recruit. Keep in mind that letters must be addressed to a specific recruit, so their names must be provided by your sailor. You can also share the list with friends, family, church, or other social groups who may want to send a card or letter to a recruit who is not receiving mail.

Emergency Communication Procedures

In case the case of an emergency or some critical event requires you to contact your recruit, you can reach them through the American Red Cross by calling 1-877-272-7337 or texting "GETHEROCARE" to 90999. You can also reach them through an online form. For more information, please visit www.redcross.org/get-help/military-families/emergency-communication.html.

05. Boot Camp Information

Recruit Training Timeline

Boot camp typically lasts for 10 weeks. During this time, your loved one will learn a wide range of skills and overcome many challenges. The following is a basic overview of what your recruit can expect, although this timeline may not exactly represent your recruit's actual journey due to any number of potential delays.

P-Days – In-Processing

Upon arrival at RTC, your recruit will have the opportunity to make a brief phone call from their cell phone to inform you of their safe arrival. Another phone call will not be permitted until about two weeks later.

During their first week, your recruit will undergo medical, dental, and fitness screening, as well as a pregnancy and drug test. Men will receive a haircut, while women can choose to keep their hair length or have it cut. They will also be taught how to style their hair according to Navy standards.

Additionally, they will meet their Recruit Division Commander, who will oversee their training and instruction. Uniforms will be issued, and your recruit will be instructed on how to wear, fold, and store them. They will also be assigned their ship and bunk, which will serve as their home during their time at RTC.

Recruits will participate in an orientation briefing and learn how to march, drill, and other basic boot camp skills.

Phase 1 – Indoctrination

During weeks 2-3 after arrival, your recruit will be introduced to basic skills that they will build upon throughout boot camp. They will attend classes on naval history, customs and courtesies, and general military and professional knowledge. They will also learn watchstanding, undergo personal and material inspections, and engage in physical training. Additionally, they will take their first physical fitness test.

Recruits must also pass a swimming test. Those who cannot swim will receive training from Water Survival Instructors. Your recruit will also participate in shipboard emergency simulations with their fellow recruits.

Phase 2 – Militarization

Your recruit will begin training on a land-bound training ship. They will learn knot tying, line handling, firefighting techniques, first aid, drill, and firearms training. Physical training will continue, and they will need to pass a second academic test.

During this phase they will face the dreaded Confidence Chamber. This is a simulation of a chemical attack designed to instill confidence in their equipment. They will join other recruits in the chamber and don their gas masks. Then, a tear-gas tablet is lit. After the gas fills the chamber, the recruits will be ordered to remove their masks and recite their name and other vital information.

Phase 3 – Evaluation

During weeks 7-8, your recruit will be tested on all the skills they have learned up to this point. This will include physical fitness tests, inspections, and assessments on firefighting, line handling, and weapons.

Phase 4 – Sailor for Life

This is the final exam. Your recruit's knowledge will be tested in simulations on the USS *Trayer* training simulator. This is an intense 12-hour test that simulates getting underway on a ship and reacting to an attack at sea. Many of the scenarios they will encounter are based on real-world events including the terrorist attack on the guided-missile destroyer USS *Cole* in 2000, the 1990 mine damage to amphibious assault ship USS *Tripoli*, and the 1987 Iran-Iraq war missile attack on USS *Stark*.

To graduate, recruits must score 80 or higher on this exam. If they pass, they will participate in a capping cere-mony, where they will exchange their Recruit ball cap for a Navy ball cap, signifying their transition to a U.S. Navy Sailor.

Although your loved one is now a U.S. Navy Sailor, their testing is not yet complete. They will be required to pass a final Physical Readiness Test and participate in clas-ses on small unit leadership, professional development, and fleet and shipboard living.

Week 10 marks the culmination of your sailor's hard work and training during boot camp. They will participate in the graduation ceremony known as Pass in Review or PIR, and hopefully, you will be able to celebrate this achievement with them.

Phone Call Schedule

How often your sailor will be able to make phone calls, and for how long, can be determined by a wide range of variables. I have included the timeline based on the infor-mation provided on the official Navy website at www.bootcamp.navy.mil/Recruits. However, this can be altered by how long it takes your sailor to be assigned a di-vision, when they actually start training, and their division's performance. Their RDC may also add or remove phone calls privileges based solely on their discretion. If a phone call is not received during this timeline, do not assume the worst. When it comes to boot camp, no news is good news, even if they aren't granted phone call privileges due to per-formance issues.

Arrival Phone Call

This will be a brief phone call, essentially telling you

they have arrived, and they are safe. There won't be any time to talk. Tell them that you love them, support them, and have confidence in their success.

Phone Call 1

Your first real phone call comes at the end of Phase 1. This will usually be around the second or third week after arrival. Your recruit may be feeling overwhelmed so try to be encouraging and resist the temptation to talk too much about how much they are missed.

Phone Call 2

During Phase 2 they may be granted a phone call around week 4. They will have been doing a lot more hands-on training and are probably going to have some stories.

Phone Call 3

During Phase 3, near the end of week 7 you may get another call. This will be just before Battle Stations 21. They will be nervous, and excited, and they are one step away from getting their Navy ball cap.

Phone Call 4

This is the "I'm a Sailor" call! Your recruit has just become a proud member of the U.S. Navy. Be prepared to be excited. However, there is a small chance they did not pass Battle Stations 21. You will want to allow them to vent frustration and disappointment but encourage them and express your unwavering support and confidence in their ability to succeed when they try again.

You may not get another call opportunity, so address any lingering questions about PIR now.

Additional Calls

If their RDC allows them, your sailor may get additional opportunities to call. Hopefully all of your questions about your trip and plans for PIR are already resolved so you can just enjoy talking to them again. Enjoy the time and remember to celebrate their accomplishments!

Roles and Ranks at Boot Camp

The Recruit Division Commander (RDC) will assign leadership roles to recruits. These roles are important in helping your recruit gain leadership knowledge and experience. However, they don't carry over to any other rank or role after boot camp, and don't mean any increase in pay or benefits.

That said, holding a role like RCPO during their training and doing well at it, can lead to being singled out for Honor Recruit or Honor Graduates and other awards.

The following outlines the command structure of a training division. This list only includes the higher tiers of Recruit Petty Officers that will be common in most divisions. Some divisions may have additional roles that may be filled.

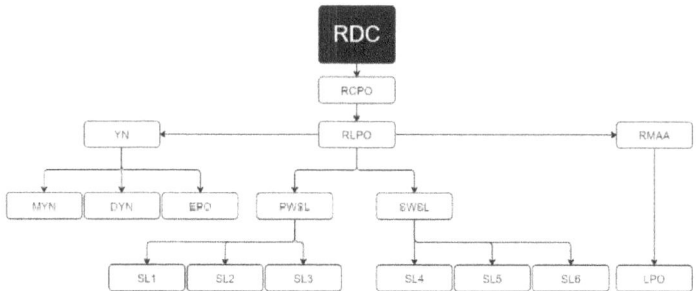

RDC (Recruit Division Commander): The RDC is the person responsible for training the recruits. The RDC will appoint Recruit Petty Officers. All RPO positions below are held by recruits.

- **RCPO (Recruit Chief Petty Officer):** The primary recruit assistant to the RDC. They are often referred to as the RPOC. You can spot the RCPO during PIR as they will be standing in front of the division and carrying a sword.

- ○ **RLPO (Recruit Leading Petty Officer):** Assists the RCPO in ensuring compliance and will assume RCPO duties when required. This used to be called Assistant Recruit Chief Petty Officer (AROC). AROC is still used as shorthand for this role. To keep the recruits in step while marching, the AROC will callout the cadences.

  - ▪ **PWSL (Port Watch Section Leader):** The senior Recruit Petty Officer responsible for the rotation of the ship watchstanders with the RDCs.

    - • **RSLPO (Recruit Section Leaders):** There are three section leaders that report to the PWSL. The Section Leaders supervise the recruits in their section and monitor the recruits' personal cleanliness, military appearance, clothing care, and watchstanding.

  - ▪ **SWSL (Starboard Watch Section Leader):** The senior Recruit Petty Officer responsible for coordinating the division's watchbill.

    - • **RSLPO (Recruit Section Leaders):** There are three section leaders that report to the SWSL. The Section Leaders supervise the recruits in their section and monitor the recruits' personal cleanliness, military appearance, clothing care, and watchstanding.

- ○ **YN (Recruit Yeoman):** Performs general clerical duties in the division and assists RDCs with preparation and maintenance of divisional reports, records, class attendance rosters, mail pick-up and distribution.

  - ▪ **MYN (Recruit Medical Yeoman) RPO2:** The Recruit Medical Yeoman prepares and maintains the medical documentation for recruits. They also coordinate appointments with the medical liaison and track the status of all physicals. They will also attend a medical/dental brief.

- **DYN (Recruit Dental Yeoman) RPO2:** The DYN assists in preparing and maintaining the dental documentation for recruits. They will also coordinate appointments with the dental liaison, track the status of all special exams, and attend a medical/dental brief.

- **EPO (Recruit Education Petty Officer):** The EPO is responsible for administering and mustering mandatory and night study.

○ **RMAA (Recruit Master-at-Arms):** This recruit reports to the RCPO and RDC and is responsible for the cleanliness and upkeep of the division spaces. In the absence of the RDC, RCPO, and the RLPO.

- **LPO (Division Laundry Petty Officer) RPO2:** The LPO is responsible for the execution of proper laundry handling procedures. They will also maintain the cash box and division expense log.

Competitive Flags

Divisions who excel at specific performance goals are awarded recognition flags. They carry these flags proudly as a symbol of their success. Every test, assessment, drill, or inspection has a possible score of 5 for the recruits individually, and as a division. The best performing division will be honored at PIR.

Scholastic Flag

This is a white flag with a red "S". This flag is awarded

to a division that receives a 4.0 or higher on the academic test.

Drill Flag

This is a white flag with a rifle and a sword crossed on it. This is awarded for receiving a 4.0 on drill assessment.

Compartment Readiness

This is a white flag with a blue star inside a yellow circle. It is awarded for obtaining a 4.0 average in compartment cleanliness.

Physical Fitness Flag

This is a white flag with a blue "A" inside a yellow circle. It is awarded to 3.5 on the first physical assessment and a 4.0 on the second.

Battle Efficiency Flag

This is a yellow and blue flag with a white letter "E" inside the central blue stripe. This flag is awarded for excellence in every phase of training. The Battle Efficiency Honor Division Recognition is bestowed on the division who has an overall average of 4.35.

Captain's Cup Olympics Flag

This is a red flag with gold rings (they look like the Olympic rings. This is awarded to the division that wins the most events at the Captain's Cup competition. Divisions compete in multiple athletic competitions such as push-ups, pull-ups, firefight equipment relay, and some more traditional sports such as basketball volleyball, and softball throwing.

Awards

Six individual Honor Recruits will be awarded at the graduation ceremony for their achievements. Families of the winners will be notified via letter 1-2 weeks prior to PIR. The award winners will also be posted on the RTC website.

Award winners will receive a commemorative token

from the commanding officer in recognition of their achievement. Furthermore, guests of the award winners will be seated in a reserve section during PIR. Following the ceremony, Honor Recruits and their families will attend a private reception.

Academic Excellence Award

This is awarded to the recruit with the highest overall academic score throughout all phases of training.

Navy League Award

Awarded to the recruit displaying extraordinary qualities best expressing the American spirit of honor. This recruit displays enthusiasm, a supportive attitude and a willingness to help others.

United Services Organization Shipmate Award

The recruit awarded the United Services Organization Shipmate award best exemplifies the spirit and intent of the word shipmate.

Military Order of the World Wars Award of Merit

This award is presented to the recruit for meritorious performance during recruit training.

Military Officers Association of America Award

Awarded to the recruit for demonstrating exceptional tenacity and professionalism.

Navy Club of the United States Military Excellence Award

This award is presented to the pinnacle of the graduating sailors. This is the highest award a recruit can earn.

06. Planning for PIR

Each family will need to plan for their trip in a manner that will be best suited to their needs. Travel, accommodations, and how long you can actually spend in Illinois will be different for everyone. The lists below include a basic set of items to consider.

1. Secure Transportation to Great Lakes

2. Secure transportation while in Illinois (i.e. rental car, ride share, taxi, or shuttles).

3. Secure a place to stay. We recommend the Navy Lodge for small groups of 4 or less. Air BnB is a better option for larger groups.

4. Arrangements for pets.

Packing List

On top of packing for your own needs, consider the following list regarding things for your sailor:

1. **Favorite Underwear.** Sounds silly, but some underwear is more comfortable than others. If you sailor wants to rest in the hotel room, they will wish they had these.

2. **Comfy Shoes:** If your sailor has a favorite shoe, crocks, or slippers, pack them. The only shoes they will be wearing will not be great for relaxing.

3. **Sleepwear:** Your sailor may want to rest and nap, or even lounge around in pajamas. They don't take up a lot of space, so pack their favorite.

4. **Loungewear:** Comfortable clothing like sweatpants, hoodies or sweaters, or a favorite shirt are a great thing to pack in case your sailor wants to rest

in the hotel room. Remember, they can only wear their uniform while in public, but in the privacy of a hotel room they can wear whatever they want.

5. **Sentimental/Important Item:** Pack at least one sentimental or important item from home that is easily transportable. A portable game console, a favorite stuffed animal, favorite blanket, or a small musical instrument will bring a warm smile to their face and remind them of home. It's wonderful to watch their faces light up when they see these important pieces of home brought to them.

6. **Any Letters, Cards, Personal Sentiments:** There's a pretty good chance family and friends have sent or brought you cards or other sentiments, gifts, and more. Bring only what is reasonable to pack. Like the sentimental item, it will be a nice surprise for them to see all the love and support that was meant for them back home. It's also not a bad idea to reach out to family or close friends and ask if there is anything they may want you to deliver to your sailor. Your sailor probably won't be able to take any of these with them to "A" School, but they will enjoy seeing them. It's also nice to take pictures of their reaction to these sentiments. You can text them to the loved one or friend who sent them.

07. Pass In Review

The information below was sourced from official Navy websites. For current PIR policy, rules, and schedules you should also visit www.bootcamp.navy.mil/graduation.

Tickets for PIR

- Only 3-4 guests are permitted to PIR. Keep in mind that this is subject to change, and guest allowances may be more restricted.

- The recruit will decide who is added to the guest list. Be sure you communicate with your recruit early regarding who to add to the guest list. I recommend providing a list in order of priority before the recruit leaves for RTC. Update that list via letters if any person is not going to be able to make it. Keep in mind that if attendance is restricted to three or fewer guests then the names at the top of the list have priority. Be sure the list is correct before the final week of training.

- A security form will be mailed to you regarding PIR. Follow the instructions on that letter CAREFULLY.

- Recruits can't trade seats. If a recruit only has two guests coming, they can't give another recruit the remaining seats.

- Do not call or request additional seats. You get what you get and no special treatment under any circumstances will be considered.

PIR Date Schedule

- 6:30 am: RTC gate opens to guests.

- 7:00 am: Ceremonial drill hall doors open to guests.

- 8:45 am: All guests must be seated. Ceremonial drill hall doors close, no further entry for guests.

- 9:00 am: Graduation Ceremony commences.

- 9:20 am: Divisions arrive.

- 10:30 am: The Graduation Ceremony concludes.

Leave early to arrive early. This seems like a nobrainer but consider that many people will arrive unprepared as early as you are thinking to leave and can slow things down. We arrived nearly an hour early.

Remember to bring your PIR event tickets and a valid ID (see below) for each guest. Have them ready at the gate. This is one of those things that slows people down. They start pulling out the required documents when pulling up to the guards instead of already having them in hand when they pull up. The best solution is to have everyone holding their correct documentation before entering the car or leaving for PIR. They can hold onto it for the few minutes it takes to get to the base.

- **For visitors 18 and up** you must bring a valid government issued photo identification such as your driver's license, state ID card, passport, military ID card.

- **For visitors 17 and under** you must bring one of the following government issued photo identification cards listed above, or a valid school ID, driver's permit, copy of their birth certificate, or social security card.

Alternative Routes

Many GPS routes to the event will instruct you toward using Hwy 137/Buckley Rd. While this is technically correct, you will likely run into some congestion, especially at the turn into Navy RTC. The following routes provide an alternative that may reduce your actual travel time by bypassing the traffic.

My wife found these directions on Facebook, but they were actually sourced from www.mynavytaxi.com. I have clarified them using common GPS maps such as Google and Bing Maps. Use the directions that correspond to your relative location to the event. If you have the time the night before, try driving the route from where you are staying so that you have a good idea of the time frame. Furthermore, you will be able to plan and accommodate for any construction or road closures that may exist. However long the trip may take, add 15-30 minutes to your travel time to the event. You will still need to use the same security gate as everyone else and additional traffic or other unforeseen issues you may encounter during your drive.

From the North

1. Take either Green Bay Road, Hwy 41/Skokie Hwy, or Hwy 43/Waukegan Road south to 22nd St/Martin Luther King Jr. Dr. The specific highway you take to reach Martin Luther King Jr. Dr. will be based on your proximity.

2. Turn left onto 22nd St/Martin Luther King Jr Dr

3. Head east and continue past Commonwealth Ave.

4. Turn right onto Hwy 137/Bobby E. Thompson

Expy/Hiawatha Pioneer Trl/Lakefront Hwy

5. Stay in the left lane and continue about ¾ of a mile.

6. You will see the train station (Ohio Street). Continue in the left lane until you reach the gate.

From the South

1. Take either Hwy 131/Green Bay Road, Hwy 41/Skokie Highway, or Hwy 43/Waukegan Road north to Marting Luther King Jr Dr. Note that GPS directions from these roads will tell you to continue to Buckley Rd. While this is the most direct course, Buckley Road will have a lot of traffic for the event. Follow the steps below to bypass this congestion.

2. Turn right onto 22nd St/Martin Luther King Jr Dr

3. Head east for about 1 mile. Continue past Commonwealth Ave.

4. Turn right onto Hwy 137/Bobby E. Thompson Expy/Hiawatha Pioneer Trl/Lakefront Highway

5. Stay in the left lane and continue about ¾ of a mile.

6. You will see the train station (Ohio Street). Continue in the left lane until you reach the gate.

From the West

1. Take Buckley Rd East toward Hwy 41/Skokie Highway.

2. Turn left onto Hwy 41/Skokie Highway.

3. Turn right onto 22nd St/Martin Luther King Jr Dr

4. Head east for about 1 mile. Continue past Commonwealth Ave.

5. Turn right onto Bobby E. Thompson Expy/Hiawatha Pioneer Trl/Lakefront Highway/Hwy 137

6. Stay in the left lane and continue about ¾ of a mile.

7. You will see the train station (Ohio Street). Continue in the left lane until you reach the gate.

From Navy Lodge Great Lakes

1. Head north on Meridian Dr toward Pacific Rd

2. Turn right onto Cavin Dr

3. Turn left onto IL-131/N Green Bay Rd

4. Turn right onto 22nd St/Martin Luther King Jr Dr

5. Head east for about 1 mile. Continue past Commonwealth Ave.

6. Turn right onto Bobby E. Thompson Expy/Hiawatha Pioneer Trl/Lakefront Highway/Hwy 137

7. Stay in the left lane and continue about ¾ of a mile.

8. You will see the train station (Ohio Street). Continue in the left lane until you reach the gate.

Security Information

All persons entering are subject to searches. Visitors will pass through metal detectors and have their bags searched. Do not bring any of the following:

- Large bags, backpacks, luggage
- Posters, signs/banners
- Gift bags of any size
- Flowers
- Alcohol
- Illegal drugs
- Knives or weapons

The following items are allowed:

- Small bag/personal item (purse, satchel, etc.)

- small diaper bag

- small camera bag

- personal wheelchair or walker

- Strollers and car seats are allowed but discouraged due to space restrictions.

Be aware of the guards and their instructions. We have seen absent-minded visitors ignoring instructions by guards. These can be interpreted as a security risk, so always pay attention to the armed guards and anything they are saying or doing. I witnessed some drivers parking in front of the NEX along the roadway into the base. One driver was not aware of the guards shouting for them to move their vehicle. The guards were getting noticeably tense by having their orders ignored, and both their posture and voices were getting more aggressive. Eventually the constant shouting got the driver's attention and they proceeded onward with an apologetic wave.

This tension is not simply a matter of frustration with being ignored. They take security very seriously and must consider anyone ignoring their instructions as a possible threat. Please respect their consideration for the safety of everyone on that base, and act accordingly.

Additional Suggestions and Tips

Try using the balcony seating. It is usually sparsely populated, and you have an excellent view of the event.

If you have back problems, consider using the top row of the bleachers. They are up against a wall so you can lean back on it.

Limit the video or pictures you take. There are no

rules against taking pictures or video. However, video of the event will be available online. The Navy is recording and live streaming the event and the quality of the video is quite good. Video taken from your phone or video recorder will simply distract you from experiencing the event unnecessarily. I recommend visiting the RTC Public Affairs YouTube channel at www.youtube.com/@RTCPublicAffairs to see the video production of past events.

Your sailor may have already ordered the DVD for the video. However, you can also order one while at PIR. After the event, go to the Photo Lab at the NEX. The DVD is mailed about 5 or 6 weeks after PIR. If you missed this opportunity, try calling the Photo Lab to see if you can order the DVD at 847-578-6205.

Be prepared to buy some souvenirs at the NEX. Navy Mom, Dad, Brother, and Sister shirts and hoodies are very popular.

08. Things to Do in Chicago

Chicago is a large and diverse city, with a wide range of exciting activities to take part in with your sailor. This list provides some ideas. Of the sites listed below, we only had time to visit Navy Pier and Millennium Park. However, the list below also includes many of the locations we talked about in planning our trip. If we are lucky enough to be able to visit Chicago in the future, we expect to visit everything else on the lists below.

Sites and Activities

Navy Pier: A 50-acre waterfront destination stretching into Lake Michigan. Navy Pier has countless shops, restaurants, boat tours, performances, a children's museum, and a 200-foot Ferris wheel! www.navypier.org

Millennium Park: Home of the cloud gate. We had a lot of fun here, despite seeing it in late fall. If you are visiting Chicago in the spring or summer, you owe it to yourself to visit this park. www.choosechicago.com/articles/parks-outdoors/millennium-park-campus/

Chicago River Tours and Cruises: The Chicago River cuts through the city. Why not take one of the many boat tours and enjoy a day on the water. You can also spend your lunch or dinner on one of the dining cruises. We didn't have an opportunity to try any specific cruises out. However, any future trips will include a dining cruise on our itinerary. www.choosechicago.com/articles/tours-and-attractions/find-the-chicago-boat-tour-for-you/

Lincoln Park Zoo: The Lincoln Park Zoo is one of the country's few remaining free-admission zoos. Founded in 1868, the 35-acre zoo is home to a wide variety of animals from over 200 species including polar bears, monkeys, gorillas, penguins and big cats. You can also view live cams of some exhibits on their website. www.lpzoo.org

Museum of Science and Industry: MSI is a large museum with over two-thousand exhibits across seventy-five halls. Some exhibits require additional fees. There are several interactive elements for kids as well. Among the attractions is a guided tour of a restored captured U505 German Submarine from World War II, the Apollo 8 Command Module, and temporary exhibits from history, science and popular culture such as Harry Potter and Star Wars. Check the website for availability, pricing, and to plan the trip (including fees for special exhibits and tours). www.msichicago.org

Wrigley Field: The historical hub of the Chicago Cubs since 1914. You may not be able to catch a game there, but there are walking tours as well. Tours include visits to dugout, Visting Clubhouse, the field and more. However, some access may be restricted if the tour is on a game day. www.mlb.com

The Chicago River Walk: This is a 2.7-mile scenic trail through Chicago with food and shopping along the way. It's a very relaxing path through the city with playscapes for kids, art, architecture, memorials, performances and events. Bicycles and pets are allowed on the River Walk. www.chicago.gov/city/en/sites/chicagoriverwalk/home.html

The Second City: The Second City is a comedy and Chicago institution. It is the oldest improvisational comedy troupe to continuously operate in the city. The list of comedians who are considered alumni of Second City is extensive, including such legends as Joan Rivers, John Belushi, and Harold Ramus. www.secondcity.com

Willis Tower Skydeck: Willis Tower (formerly known as but still referred to as the Sears Tower) is the tallest building in Chicago and the third tallest building in the western hemisphere. Visit the Willis Tower Skydeck which has an interactive museum, dining options, and fifty-mile view that extends out to Lake Michigan, Chicago, and three other states from a glass balcony extending over four feet from the side of the tower. The quality of the view and the experience may be affected by visibility and the weather, so plan accordingly. www.theskydeck.com

Dining

The section includes only dining experiences we personally enjoyed. Consider these recommendations. However, they are completely reliant on personal taste. Chicago is a city with so many great opportunities for great dining experiences. I actually hesitated on including a list of restaurants for fear of excluding all the wonderful places we would not enjoy. However, the places below were such a great part of our Chicago experience I felt obligated to include them.

Egg Harbor Cafe: My personal favorite meal of our trip. Egg Harbor Café had a great atmosphere and fantastic food. There is a location in Lake Forest between RTC and Chicago, which makes it a great stop after picking up your sailor if you intend to visit the city. www.eggharborcafe.com

Create Your Own Cheesecake & Cheesesteak (CYOC): Our first stop for lunch with our sailor after PIR We enjoyed both the cheesesteak sandwiches and the huge variety of cheesecakes. https://www.cyocinc.com/

Potbelly: Potbelly is a sandwich chain established in 1977 in the Lincoln Park neighborhood of Chicago. They have grown to over 250 locations. We don't have any in Florida, but we tried one during our trip. This is a great option for food that is made quickly, but is not fast food.

www.potbelly.com

Starbucks Reserve: 5 floors of coffee and baked goods. The rooftop terrace is a nice place to relax and enjoy a cup with the family. But be prepared for crowds. www.starbucksreserve.com

Giordano's: I'm sure there are Chicago natives who can probably give me a strong argument for better Chicago-style pizzas, but we didn't have access to any personally known Chicagolanders. Giordano's might be a national chain now, but they started in Chicago, and are an Illinois institution. The specific restaurant we went to near the Navy Lodge was packed full of patrons, which should give anyone confidence in its quality. We picked up a few pies and enjoyed them very much. Lucky for us, there are some locations in Florida we will be visiting soon. www.giordanos.com.

09. Guide to Departure Day

Many graduates will leave by plane via Chicago's O'Hare International Airport. This is an opportunity to spend even more time with your Sailor before they depart for "A" School. In 2004 the Transportation Security Administration (TSA) issued TSA Security Directive 1544-01-10w. This allows for military passenger family members to enter the area of the airport defined as the Sterile Concourse with a special access pass. Guests must process through the ticket line and TSA checkpoints with their military passenger. While not all airports or airlines are capable of issuing this pass, it is accessible at O'Hare.

Families should keep in mind that the time allotted will depend entirely on when your sailor's flight will depart, and it won't be possible to learn that time until they have arrived at the airport and checked in. Families should also expect their sailor to be very active during this time. You will spend quite a bit of your time running from gate to gate so that your sailor can say farewell to friends from boot camp. O'Hare is a large airport, and departures will be across a great many different gates, airlines, and at various times.

The following list provides information and tips for spending departure day with your sailor.

1. Setup a family group text (if you don't already have one) for communication on that day. Agree with all participants to use this text group for all communications for Departure Day.

2. Pack all necessary medical equipment and prescriptions into a small, easy to handle, bag. Note that you will need to go through TSA security screening. Do not pack anything that would not be permitted to take on a plane. DO NOT pack food, toiletry

supplies, or large gifts. Everything brought with you must comply with TSA restrictions. For a full list of what can and can't be brought please check the TSA website or click the following link: www.tsa.gov/travel/security-screening/whatcanibring

3. You will need your photo ID, driver's license, passport or some other identification in order to get a visitor's pass at O'Hare.

4. Be prepared to spend some money. Eating at the airport isn't cheap. While they do have some fast-food and cheap options, they can still have elevated prices. You should budget for three meals per person at $15-$50 per person depending on your preferences.

5. Be prepared for a message by 5AM on the morning of departure day. Your recruit will need to text you once they are ready to board the buses.

6. Once at O'Hare, park in any available spaces in Terminal 2.

7. Follow signs to proceed to the Departures floor (this should be the ground floor). Alternatively, you can try to find the bus drop off, but this is unnecessary.

8. Wait for your sailor to arrive. Once they depart the bus, they will be gathered in a waiting area with their luggage to wait for their formal orders and paperwork. While they wait for orders, they can text you with information on where they are located.

9. After their orders are received, they will gather at a check-in desk. YOU MUST CHECK IN WITH THEM in order to get a visitor pass into O'Hare. They recruit will check their luggage and get their

boarding passes, and you and any other family members staying with your sailor at O'Hare will get your visitor passes.

10. Finally, you will go through TSA security. Once inside the concourse area, you won't be coming back through security again until after your sailor's departure.

O'Hare Resources

Here are some other resources that may be helpful on your day at O'Hare:

- O'Hare Airport Terminal Map: www.chicago-ohare-airport.com/map

- Eating and Shopping Guide: www.flychicago.com/ohare/eatshopmore

- TSA Security Screening : www.tsa.gov/travel/security-screening

10. Terms

Navy recruits will start using an entirely new language when talking to you. Here are some terms that can be helpful.

"A" School: Accession Training. This is where sailors are given the technical training required to perform their job.

ASMO (Assignment Memorandum): refers to getting set back in training or getting kicked out. You won't get kicked out unless for medical reasons (including mental health). Otherwise, ASMO is used as a term describing being recycled into another division. Like being held back a grade.

ASVAB (Armed Services Vocational Aptitude Battery): A multiple choice test used to determine qualification for enlistment in the Armed Forces. This test can also determine eligibility for different occupations, based on score requirements in each section of the ASVAB.

Battle Stations: A 12-hour intense training exam simulating an attack at sea on board a replica of a guided missile destroyer. Some scenarios are modeled after real-life events faced by Sailors aboard the USS Cole, USS Tripoli, USS Forestall and USS Stark. This is the Sailor's final exam. After passing Battle Stations, they will take part in a capping ceremony. They will exchange their Navy ballcaps with the word "Recruit" stitched across it for a new ballcap stitched with the word "Sailor". This can be a highly emotional moment for your sailor.

Cadence: A kind of rhythmic chant or song used to help recruits keep time during marches.

Compartment: This is the living space of sailors including the bunk spaces, bathroom, and shower area.

Division: This is a training group made up of Sections. A division is supervised by 3 RDCs. There are competitive, but friendly, rivalries between divisions.

Liberty: Basically, this is time off.

MEPS (Military Entrance Processing Station): Stations which screen and process applicants for military service. Applicants are required to submit and pass numerous medical, social, psychological and vocational tests (such as the ASVAB). They will then meet with a service counselor to negotiate and sign enlistment contracts and swear (or affirm) an entrance oath.

OPFA (Official Physical Fitness Assessment): Physical fitness tests with standards the recruit must meet. Failure to meet these requirements may result in being ASMO'd.

NEX (Navy Exchange): The NEX is shorthand for the Navy Exchange retail stores operated by the NEXCOM on and near Navy bases for use by active military, retired military, and some civilians. During RTC, there is a special section of the NEX where recruits can purchase personal hygiene products and other goods. Following the PIR ceremony, the families often congregate on NEX on base. You can also purchase souvenirs.

NEXCOM (Navy Exchange Service Command): A Department of the Navy organization that oversees seven primary business:

- Navy Exchange (NEX)

- Ship Store Program

- Uniform Program Management Office

- Navy Clothing and Textile Research Facility (NCTRF)

- Navy Lodge Program

- Navy Gateway Inns & Suites

- Telecommunications Program Office

OPSEC (Operations Security): A process used to help protect information that may be used by hostile actors. It is a good idea for families of military personal to be aware of certain OPSEC guidelines, especially when discussing their sailor on social media. Guidelines for military personal include (but are not limited to):

- Be aware the photos you take with your smartphones and load to the internet may have been geotagged.

- Be aware of information you are putting out in emails, online, phone conversations, photos and open unsecure conversations in public.

- Be aware of or disable geolocation capabilities on devices or applications.

- Don't discuss details, such as:

    o Timelines, detailed locations, or movements

    o limitations or capabilities

    o Specific names, ranks, job titles, or budgets

    o Current or future operations

    o Security procedures

PIR (Pass in Review): This is the graduation ceremony for Navy sailors before they proceed to "A" School.

P-Days (Processing Days): This is the 5 business days prior to actual training where the recruit will be organized into divisions, assigned roles, and be trained in basic expectations during boot camp. While going through P-Days the recruits will be housed in Ship 1. Following P-Days they are moved to their actual ship and begin training.

PERSEC (Personal/Personnel Security): Similar to OPSEC, this focuses specifically on protecting the individual sailor. The best practice for loved ones is to refrain from publicly posting information about your sailor, such as their full name, personal information such as phone numbers and addresses, or any other personal information that can be traced back to your or your sailor.

PRT (Physical Readiness Test): A physical test to determine the physical fitness of Navy personnel.

Racks: Racks are bunk beds. A recruit is assigned to one bed. The recruit assigned to the other bed is a Rack Mate. Rack mats hold each other accountable for the state of their bunk and storage.

Rate/Rating: Rate is usually the sailor's pay grade and rating is often their occupation in the Navy. However, we heard sailors referring to "rate" in both contexts. When a sailor asks another sailor what their rate is, they are usually asking what their occupation or job is. They usually refer to them using abbreviations such as MC1 for Mass Communication Specialist 1st Class.

RDC (Recruit Division Commander): One of 3 people supervising a division.

Recruit: This is the enlistee before they pass Battle Stations. Recruits wear a Navy ballcap with the word "Recruit" stitched on it.

RTC (Recruit Training Command): The official designation for boot camp. RTC is a command unit within the

United States Navy that is primarily responsible for the initial training of recruits.

Sandboxx: An app used for connecting with sailors.

Section: One of six groups of recruits that make up a division.

Separated/Separation: This means the recruit or sailor will be removed from the Navy. Separation may be voluntary or involuntary, meaning the recruit or sailor chooses to be separated, or the Navy is forcing the separation. Separation from the Navy may mean the individual has unfulfilled service obligations. They may be called up in the case of a national emergency or war to fulfil their obligation.

Ship: The entire training group (all divisions that will graduate together) live in a building referred to as a ship. Each division may have a bunk area in the ship with another division (called a brother or sister division). The bunks are segregated by gender.

- Ship 1 USS Pearl Harbor
- Ship 2 USS Reuben James
- Ship 3 USS Hopper
- Ship 4 USS Arleigh Burke
- Ship 5 USS Theodore Roosevelt
- Ship 6 USS Constitution
- Ship 7 USS Chicago
- Ship 9 USS John F Kennedy
- Ship 10 USS Enterprise
- Ship 11 USS Kearsarge

- Ship 12 USS Triton

- Ship 13 USS Marvin Shields

- Ship 14 USS Arizona

- Ship 17 USS Mason

Training Group: The collection of divisions who are graduating together.

Acknowledgements

This book would not have been possible without the support of my family. My wife is my biggest supporter, and my most vocal critic. You can thank her for all of the horrible writing that was exorcised from this manuscript and blame me entirely for what I kept regardless of her advice.

To my youngest daughter, I want to apologize. Her bedroom, where she is supposed to be doing schoolwork, is precariously close to my office. I'm sorry for being a horrible distraction. My frequent request to read a finished draft or to help me choose between one bit of text over another were received patiently and enthusiastically. But I think I might have been the source of some delays to her homework.

I can't really acknowledge my son's help with this book. He is working hard for the Air Force, and we are extremely proud of him! I do hope he reads the audiobook.

I also want to thank Joshua Garza and Kevin Ramdial who worked in our local recruiting office. Thank you for listening to me and helping me to get in touch with additional parents and families to both help them in the beginning of their love ones' Navy journey, and for those family's help in fleshing out some of the more ambiguous areas of the process so that I could better expand on them.

Thank you, Lieutenant Commander Harold Johnson, USNSCC, USMC Ret. He is the commanding officer and instructor of the United States Naval Sea Cadet Corps Freedom Battalion. My daughter attended four years of this program during her high school career. I have no doubts that Johnson's support and instruction were instrumental in our sailor's success at boot camp. I encourage any student who attends a school with a Sea Cadet or ROTC program to give them a chance, even if a military career is not in their plans. For more information and to see if a Sea Cadet program is available in your area, please visit www.seacadets.org.

Most of all, I want to thank my eldest daughter, the middle child, and our sailor for taking us all on this journey. Despite her crazy schedule at NNPSTC she found the time to help answer and clarify my questions and review my work. Her hard work, perseverance, determination, and wonderfully bright spirit are an inspiration to all of us.

Grace, we are so proud of you! I love you!

About the Author

Ruel Knudson was born and raised in Orlando, Florida. He currently lives there with his wife and youngest daughter. His two eldest children are currently enlisted in the U.S. Air Force and the U.S. Navy.

Ruel has been writing for most his life. Most recently he has published 3 fiction novellas. This is his first non-fiction book.

Inscriptions

If you were given this book by a recruiter and plan to pass it along to other families, please consider adding your sailor's name, PIR date, and their RTC Ship and Division to the list on the following page, along with a brief note to the family who may receive this generous donation.

Please, don't feel bad if you plan to keep this book as a memento of your family's journey and your loved one's accomplishment. However, if you are in a position to help another family, please consider ordering a copy of this book to give back to your recruiter and add your sailor's information and a message in that copy.

Sailor's Last Name _____

PIR Date _____

Ship Name and # _____

Division _____

Message _____

_____

_____

_____

_____

Sailor's Last Name _____

PIR Date _____

Ship Name and # _____

Division _____

Message _____

_____

_____

_____

_____

Sailor's Last Name _____

PIR Date _____

Ship Name and # _____

Division _____

Message _____

_____

_____

_____

_____

Sailor's Last Name _____

PIR Date _____

Ship Name and # _____

Division _____

Message _____

_____

_____

_____

_____

Sailor's Last Name _____
PIR Date _____
Ship Name and # _____
Division _____
Message _____
_____
_____
_____
_____

Sailor's Last Name _____
PIR Date _____
Ship Name and # _____
Division _____
Message _____
_____
_____
_____
_____

Sailor's Last Name _____
PIR Date _____
Ship Name and # _____
Division _____
Message _____
_____
_____
_____
_____

Sailor's Last Name _____
PIR Date _____
Ship Name and # _____
Division _____
Message _____
_____
_____
_____
_____

Visit

For additional resources, exclusive content, supplemental material, and updates related to "Underway: One Family's Guide to Surviving Boot Camp," visit our website at www.underwaybook.com. Dive deeper into the journey through boot camp, PIR, and more!

Connect

Join the growing community on Facebook! Follow as at www.facebook.com/underway.book for discussions, behind-the-scenes insights, and more.

Explore

If you're a fan of fiction, dark westerns, gothic fantasy, horror, or post-apocalyptic adventure don't miss out! Check out my other captivating books at www.ruelknudson.com.

www.ingramcontent.com/pod-product-compliance
Lightning Source LLC
Chambersburg PA
CBHW082104140626
46553CB00018B/633